Single Adults

George Barna

Issachar Resources
A Division of Barna Research Group, Ltd.
Ventura, California

Published by Issachar Resources, a division of the Barna Research Group,
Ltd., 5528 Everglades Street, Ventura, CA 93003. All rights reserved. No
portion of this book may be reproduced, stored in a retrieval system or
transmitted in any form or by any means - electronic, mechanical, photo-
copy, computer scan, recording or any other - except for brief quotations
in printed reviews, without the prior written permission of the publisher or
author.

All Scripture quotations in this book, except where noted otherwise, are
from the Holy Bible: New International Version.
Copyright © 1973, 1978, 1984 by International Bible Society. Used by
permission of Zondervan Publishing House. All Rights Reserved.

Library of Congress Cataloging-in-Publication Data
Barna, George
Single Adults / George Barna

‾‾‾‾‾‾‾‾‾‾‾‾‾‾‾
ISBN 0-9671372-4-1

Printed in Canada

ACKNOWLEDGMENTS

Here's my confession. Even though I have written a book about single adults, I am married – and have been for 23 years, which is a long time removed from living as a bachelor. I have never experienced a divorce – okay, on some days it seemed like a better alternative than staying married, but I resisted the impulse – and my parents never got divorced, either, so I do not have any personal experience with being single through divorce. If the probabilities hold true, my wife will outlive me, so I won't know what widowhood is like, either. What this boils down to is that the only thing that qualifies me to write this book is the extensive research that my company—the Barna Research Group—and I have conducted among single adults on a wide range of topics. It is my fervent hope that single adults are able to adequately and accurately tell you their story through the research.

Not only can I not claim to have personal knowledge of what it's like to be single these days by virtue of being unmarried, but I cannot even take sole credit for the research about our subjects. I am blessed with a terrific team of professionals with whom I have the honor of working. You should know who they are. In alphabetical order (I feared there might be a backlash if I listed them chronologically) they are: Rachel Ables, Jim Fernbaugh, Meg Flammang, Lynn Gravel, Cameron Hubiak, Pam Jacob, David Kinnaman, Carmen Moore, Julie Oxenreider, Dan Parcon, Celeste Rivera, Irene Castillo, and Kim Wilson. The Lord has blessed me with a great group of people – folks who love Jesus, who are committed to His work, and who are capable professionals. It is a joy to work with them and to see how God directs our efforts.

That is my primary internal team. I thank God for them, am grateful for their continued patience with my own faults and idiosyncrasies, and am humbled that they remain passionate about the vision that God has entrusted to us in relation to His purposes.

And then there is my external team. Included in that group are the pastors of my home churches – Larry DeWitt and Larry Osborne – who, along with the staffs and lay ministers, fortify us with their prayers and ministry. Developing resource materials for ministries has become an act of spiritual warfare, and it is the prayers and encouragement of these spiritual warriors that sustain us.

Sealy Yates, Curtis Yates and John Eames are also on the external team as my literary agents. How wonderful it is to have trustworthy and competent professionals who genuinely care about me, my ministry and their role in furthering that outreach.

And, of course, there is my personal team: my family. They are God's unique and special blessing to me. About two decades ago my wife, Nancy, helped launch Barna Research, and has guided it from day one to financial stability and operational nimbleness. She takes on greater responsibility during my frenetic writing periods, handling the increased load with great aplomb. My daughters Samantha and Corban have been endlessly loving, forgiving and enjoyable. With every book I write they sacrifice time that I should be spending with them, so that I may have the opportunity to communicate truths that (we hope) will bless and help people. They deserve magnificent blessings for all they do to enable books like this to emerge.

Finally, I must thank the Lord Himself for continuing to find a use for me in His kingdom. I would have been tired of my nonsense by now if I were Him, but I suppose that's one of the zillion reasons why He is God and I am not. May this book honor and glorify Him and be useful in the pursuit of His purposes and in the development of His kingdom. What a privilege it is to know Him, to love Him and to serve Him.

George Barna
February 2002

TABLE OF CONTENTS

Chapter 1
YOU'RE NOT ALONE
IF YOU'RE SINGLE

Did you know that in four states you may legally get married at age 12?

If you guessed that the European nations often described as the sex capitals of the world, such as Denmark and Holland, have the highest divorce rates on earth, you would be exactly – wrong. The United States holds that dubious distinction.

Were you aware that there are more widowed people in the U.S. than the entire populations of more than four dozen nations of the world, including Belgium, Bolivia, the Czech Republic, Denmark, Ecuador, Greece, Guatemala, Hungary, Ireland, Israel, New Zealand, Norway, Portugal, and Sweden?

Although many women complain about the lack of single men, did you know that there are 2 million more males who have never been married than there are never-married females?

You may realize that more than four out of five Americans call themselves Christian, and that the Christian faith discourages divorce, but have you heard that born again adults have the same likelihood of seeing their marriage end in divorce as do non-Christians?

Would you be surprised to learn that the United States has more single adults than any other nation in the world except for China and India; or that the number of singles in the U.S. exceeds the total national population of all but 11 of the world's 192 nations?[1]

How shocked would you be to discover that the number of single parents in the United States is greater than the entire population of Colorado and Tennessee combined?

As devastating as divorce is for most women, did you know that three-quarters of them get remarried?

At the turn of the twentieth century, just 1% of all adults were divorced. Were you aware that the figure has grown ten-fold since then?

Do you know what they call the most attractive men in singles bars? Married. (Sorry, just wanted to see if you were paying attention.)

Whether you examine their lifestyles, demographics or religious beliefs and practices, the growing population of single adults in America is full of surprises. Understanding the character of unmarried Americans is important, not just for the sake of knowledge, but in order to minister effectively both to them and alongside them.

But old impressions die hard. Many Americans – older Americans, in particular – assume that people cannot be happy and fulfilled unless they find a marriage partner or a "soul mate." In the past quarter-century, however, things have changed dramatically. Our perspectives on commitment and loyalty have changed. Methods of communication and desirable vocational skills have shifted. Personal relationships develop differently than in the past, and sexual relations apart from marriage have become common. Co-habitation, divorce and parenting by grandparents have skyrocketed. Tolerance of different, non-traditional lifestyles has increased. More than ever before, Americans seek the benefits of intimate relationships without the pressures and perceived limitations of marriage. That helps to explain why people wait longer – and experiment more broadly and creatively – with a spectrum of relationships and lifestyles.

It is common for novels, televisions programs, contemporary music, movies and videos to sanction non-traditional values and family arrangements, and their influence can be seen in the transformation of the nation's thinking and behavior. The black and Hispanic populations of the U.S. are often the early – and most prolific – adopters of these new living configurations, but the record shows that the white and Asian populations waste little time in jumping on the bandwagon.

The Shift From Marriage to Singlehood[2]

	all adults 18+			whites			blacks			Hispanics		
	1980	1990	1999	1980	1990	1999	1980	1990	1999	1980	1990	1999
married	66%	62%	60%	67%	64%	62%	51%	46%	41%	66%	62%	59%
never-been-married	20	22	24	19	20	21	31	35	39	24	27	29
divorced	6	8	10	6	8	10	8	11	12	6	7	8
widowed	8	8	7	8	8	7	10	9	8	4	4	4

(NBM indicates "never-been-married")

If we limit our discussion of single adults to those who have never been married or have experienced divorce, we will overlook important segments of the singles population. With advances in health care and medicine, people are living longer than ever before, leading to the precipice of an explosion in the number of widowed adults living in the U.S. These individuals typically represent the two oldest generations in the nation, the Seniors and Builders – two groups whose moral foundations differ considerably from that of younger citizens. Adults 55 and older experience a comparatively low divorce rate, but they face a high probability of living a significant number of their twilight years as singles.

And how can we neglect single parents, a subset within two of the singles' niches already described? In many cases, these adults had children while married, yet those who had children out-of-wedlock have become the fastest-growing category of single parents. The enlightenment brought on by a seemingly endless gush of articles and special reports on the plight of children and mothers of broken marriages has had little apparent impact on curtailing the growth of this household type.

Those legally married but physically separated from their spouse comprise the final singles niche to consider. This group – sometimes referred to as "the divorced-in-waiting" – is the smallest of the singles sub-populations. For many separated individuals, this state of marital ambiguity is their prime candidate for "hell on earth," a state of confusion and uncertainty that usually solves few, if any, of their marriage problems but raises a plethora of gut-wrenching questions and challenges. The results of separation are relatively predictable, however: 97% of white women who separate from their husbands are divorced within five years of the separation. (Though not as universal, the same outcome

10

occurs for three-quarters of non-white women who undergo a separation.)[3]

In summary, then, America has five distinct singles groups: the Never-Been-Married, the Divorced, the Widowed, Single Parents and the Separated. To think that all single adults are alike, and to relate to them in an identical manner is a grievous mistake – but one often made as we lump unmarried people into a single, massive population.

The Life Cycle

Some measure of our family status can be attributed to age and life situation – what is commonly known as the "life cycle." Some of the choices we make are dictated by cultural pressure, such as the expectation of getting married while a twenty-something. Other decisions are determined by age and physiological parameters, such as having babies during those years when women are physically capable of producing them (teen years through mid-forties). Overall, many of the decisions we make are an outgrowth of this life cycle phenomenon.

Marital status is affected by the life cycle. People tend to get married (for the first time, at least) during their twenties, as they settle into a career, a geographic location and a universe of personal and organizational relationships. Eager to experience the challenges and joys of parenthood, most couples begin having their children in their mid-twenties through their mid-thirties. Economic and professional pressures, the development of divergent interests, and a variety of sexual tensions often lead to divorce, commonly occurring in the person's mid-thirties to mid-forties. Re-marriage usually occurs within a few years of the initial divorce. After a period of settling down, frequently during a person's forties, fifties, or sixties, the final phase of most people's life cycle unfolds after they reach their mid-sixties and early seventies, when occupational retirement, physical limitations and widowhood define the final life stage.

Statistics bear out these patterns. Among people 18 to 24, nearly nine out of ten (87%) have never been married. That figure drops to just one-quarter (24%) among those who are in the 25 to 44 bracket. In the 35 to 54 age group, however, divorce becomes more prevalent; more than one-third of the adults in this segment have gone through at least one divorce, and two-thirds of them remarry. The incidence of widowhood jumps once people reach 65 years of age, rising from less than one in ten among people 55 to 64 years old (and, of course, much lower percentages among even younger adults) to a whopping one-third of those who reach the traditional retirement age.

These data portray a fairly predictable course of change and challenge. As we age, new opportunities, risks and dangers await us in each life phase. For most people the early years of adulthood pose the fundamental marital challenge: whether or not to get married, with whom, and when. Once a person gets married, then within the first decade of the relationship the partners are confronted by pressures that may potentially dissolve that union – and then, for most people who get divorced, a return to the pre-marital phase of trying to determine whether or not to get married (again), with whom, and when. The final chapter of the tale typically begins as we enter our mid-sixties, at which time we begin to harbor concerns about the potential death of our marriage partner.

The Marriage Life Cycle[4]

age	never been married	divorced	widowed	separated	married
18-24	87%	1%	*	1%	13%
25-34	34	7	*	3	53
35-44	16	13	1	3	64
45-54	8	15	3	3	70
55-64	5	14	9	2	72
65+	3	5	31	1	55

Never Been Down the Aisle

In the past, there was a social stigma associated with reaching your twenties and not being married. Today, however, the median age of a first marriage has risen to 25 among women and 27 among men. Unmarried young people used to face a barrage of questioners who wanted to know, "What's taking you so long? Why aren't you married yet?" Young singles used to fear the stream of behind-the-back whispers that there must be something wrong with a person who wasn't wedded by their mid-twenties. Today, though, the magnifying glass is placed over the choices of young people who plan to get married. Now they are the ones peppered with questions, such as "What's your hurry?" or even "Why are you getting married; why not just live with the person?"

The Census Bureau informs us that among people 15 and older, the never-been-married segment is now 60 million strong – 32 million men and 28 million women.[5] About one-third of that population, however, is 20 or younger. If we limit the inquiry to people 18 and older, we're speaking of a population that is 48 million people, of which nearly half is under 25. One-quarter of the never-been-married group is 25 to 34 years old, while the remaining one-quarter is 35 or older. To demonstrate the widespread draw of marriage in our land, realize that only 4% of all people 55 or older have never ventured into a marriage. In spite of the sweeping changes that are altering our lifestyles and values, an undeniable fact remains: few Americans die without having taken a dip in the marriage pond.

Even within the never-been-married public, however, there are distinct demographic patterns. For instance, while two-thirds of all white adults in the 25 to 34-age segment have been married, less than half of the black adults in that same age group have experienced marriage. Racial identification also enters the picture in a big way. Since 1980, there has been about a respectable 11% increase in the white never-been-married contingent. However, that pales in comparison to the growth within the black (26%) and Hispanic (21%) populations. Among blacks this growth is driven by a determination to experience family apart from marriage, while the Hispanic experience is driven by the profusion of young Hispanics waiting until later ages to get married.

The Prevalence of Stable Marriages Has Dropped in the Past Half Century[6]

year	never been married	divorced	widowed	married
2000	28%	9%	6%	56%
1990	26	8	7	59
1980	26	6	7	61
1970	25	3	8	64
1960	22	2	8	68
1950	23	2	8	67

Shattered Dreams

As millions of Americans will attest, getting married and staying married are two entirely different matters. The sad reality is that roughly half of all marriages end in divorce within 15 years of the wedding day.[7] At any given time, about one out of ten adults are currently divorced. However, the proportion of adults who have been married and divorced is much higher, because a majority of those who get divorced eventually remarry. Overall, one-third of the adult population that has been married has also been through at least one divorce.[8] Among people in the 30-49 age bracket, that figure is close to half.

The average age of a person at the time of their first marriage is 26; the average age of a married person's first divorce is 34. In fact, age is firmly correlated with divorce: the younger a woman is when she gets married, the more likely the marriage is to produce a divorce. Six out of ten marriages among women who got married before their eighteenth birthday wind up in divorce, compared to just one-third among women who marry after their twentieth birthday.

It seems inevitable that in America's immediate future its citizens will be increasingly comfortable with, accepting of, and even expectant of marriages fizzling in divorce. Some researchers have posited that we have shifted out of an evolutionary period regarding divorce (when we questioned our fundamental ideas about marriage, parenting, moral values and relationships) into a revolutionary period (in which we accept divorce and other non-traditional relationships as emotionally and spiritually viable, legally valid and morally reasonable).[9] The fact remains that almost nobody enters a marriage seeking to divorce, but more and more we find that the people who go through a divorce are emotionally and morally resigned to the fact that it is a normal, if not inevitable, life experience.

Redefined Families

A century ago, relatively few single parents existed – and most of them fell into that state because of the premature death of their spouse. Birth out-of-wedlock, divorce and co-habitation were social inventions yet to gain widespread acceptance. In 1900, less than one out of every one hundred adults was a single parent of a child under 18. Today, there are more than 12 million single parents with children under 18 in their care – about 6% of all adults, and roughly one out of every three families.[10] That total has tripled since 1970. In fact, 28% of the nation's children presently live with just one of their birth parents. The implication of the growth of single parent households is that a majority of the children born this year are likely to live in a single-parent home for some period of time prior to celebrating their eighteenth birthday.

The world of single parenthood is changing. More than four out of five single parents (84%) are mothers. However, two significant trends are altering that reality. The first is the steady increase in single-parent fathers being given custody of their children. Between 1990 and 2000, the number of single-parent fathers with primary custody of children under 18 has leaped by 62%, while the growth among single-parent moms has expanded by 25%. Once thought to be detrimental to the needs of the children, recent research shows just the opposite regarding fathers filling the role of the primary post-divorce parent. Because custodial fathers tend to be older, better educated, better paid, more highly motivated to care for their children and resolved to involve the mother, a growing number of cases show single-parent fathers doing a commendable job of providing their kids with a viable home environment.

The second pattern worth noting is that a growing proportion of single parents are not divorced, but had children without being married to the birth partner. Among women who are single-parent moms, 40% were not married to the father of their child. Among men who are single-parents, 35% were not wedded to the mother of their children. Given the continued growth in births outside of marriage, and the psychological acceptance our nation has embraced with this practice, we can also expect continued growth in the number of single parents who have never been married.

The Prematurely Departed

Losing a spouse through death is not something a person needs to anticipate – until they reach their sixties. While there are tragic stories of young marrieds who suffer the premature loss of a spouse, those stories are the aberration. Less than two-tenths of one percent of all people under age 35 have been widowed and less than 2% of adults in the 35 to 54-age group are widowed. Widowhood starts to become a more realistic possibility in the mid-fifties through mid-sixties, when about 9% lose their spouse to death. But once the 65-year old threshold is reached, it becomes an ever-growing probability: 17% of adults who are 65 to 69, 26% of those 70 to 74, and 46% of people 75 or older are widowed.[11]

Widowhood is an incredibly sexist experience: four out of five adults who are single due to the death of their spouse are females. Whether this is attributable to the different priorities that men and women often embrace in life – men often develop their identity and sense of value on the basis of what they do, women on the basis of whom they love and connect with emotionally – or attributable to others causes, the fact remains that widowhood is a much more likely experience for women than men.

Because the average life span of men and women is only two years different, we are sometimes lured into thinking that the proportion of widowed individuals is likely to be similar, as well. However, nearly half of all women 65 or older are widowed (45%), compared to just one-seventh of men 65 or older (14%).[12] This becomes a shattering transition time for most widowers, entailing a massive change in lifestyle (70% of all widowed adults live alone).

Shared Demographics

If we were to make the mistake of assuming that all single adults are the same, we would actually be accurate in assigning certain assessments to any unmarried person. For instance, income levels are lower for all of the single adult segments than for the married-couple population. Single adults are considerably less likely to own the home they live in (only about half do) than are married couples (four out of five own their residence).[13] And each of the single adult segments has a lower level of educational achievement than do married couples.

For the most part, however, there are significant differences regarding virtually every demographic factor studied, and understanding the variance across the singles subgroups is crucial toward possessing a healthy and realistic view of singles.

Income levels are a good example. It is true that all singles segments have lower average incomes than do married couples, but the actual median levels for each group vary tremendously. At the low end of the spectrum are single women who have never been married; their median income level is barely above the poverty level in America! Single-parent men, on the other hand, have the highest income level, close to $40,000 annually – still a far cry from the $54,276 registered among married-couples, but distant from the edge of poverty. Single-parent women live much closer to the edge of poverty, earning an average of a bit less than $25,000 annually, suggesting that there is a great deal of financial, as well as emotional pressure they must combat day to day.[14]

Income disparities are exacerbated by racial and ethnic considerations, too. The average black married-couple has a median income of nearly $50,000, which is four times what the average black single woman makes, and three times what the typical black single-parent mother – who constitute the majority of all black mothers – earns each year. In the Hispanic community, married-couples average only about $35,000 annually, generating a smaller gap between Latinos who are married and those who are not. Of course, the same general pattern holds true, even among Hispanics: single adults make substantially less (median: $16,805, among all singles) than their married-couple counterparts.[15]

What to Look For

As we work through our research on single adults, keep in mind that this is not a static population; social and personal changes will continue to redefine not only the number of single adults, but also the nature of this population. Demographically, you may expect to see changes such as the following:

- In the next thirty years the United States will experience a doubling of the population age 65 or older. Implication: a dramatic increase in the number of widows.

- As immigration continues to increase the nation's population, and our non-white segments grow at a faster rate than the white population, the proclivity of the non-white groups to have children out-of-wedlock, plus rapid growth in divorce among blacks and widowhood among Hispanics, will reshape the singles population and its needs. Expect to hear more leaders demanding programs and services offered in different languages and using different strategic approaches to remain relevant to these growing niches.

- Various religious groups, scholars and public officials have raised awareness and public concern regarding the harsh realities of being raised in a single-parent home, and have highlighted the underlying values that lead to non-traditional family units (e.g., low commitment, low loyalty, impermanence, unpredictability, emotional discontinuity). However, the evidence indicates that people usually do what has been modeled for them. Consequently, we may anticipate continued growth and acceptance of co-habitation, births outside of marriage and divorce among young people, especially within the black and Hispanic segments of society.

- The Hispanic and Asian populations in America are quite young. As those who are second and third generation immigrants of Asian and Latino heritage reach adulthood, and as a growing percentage of them enter the retirement years, the process of acculturation will further drive rates of divorce and widowhood higher.

What Else?

Perhaps you're one of the many whose eyes glaze over at demographic statistics. "That's just numbers," you may be thinking. "What about what's going on inside of these people? They're human beings. Marriage, divorce, being widowed – there are important mindsets and experiences that give life to who these people are. The numbers are merely factoids unless they can help me learn how to love, serve and involve these people through meaningful activity. Help me get inside their heads and hearts rather than just their birth certificates and Census data."

As much as I like demographic information – yes, believe it or not, it *speaks* to me in revealing ways – you're absolutely right: there is more, *much* more to the lives of unmarried people than their demographic profile. And that's precisely what we will spend the rest of this book exploring – the self-perceptions, lifestyles, values, morals, and spiritual realities of single adults. We'll get a sense of who single adults really are, and how the three primary singles populations (i.e., never-been-married, divorced and widowed adults) differ from and mirror each other. Much of the information will come from surveys that my company, the Barna Research Group, has conducted over the past two years, entailing personal interviews on a wide variety of topics with nearly 4000 single adults randomly selected from across the nation. (To provide context, I'll often allude to interviews among more than 4000 married adults we surveyed.)

Let's start the process of understanding single adults more deeply by exploring how they describe themselves...

Footnotes

[1] Those eleven nations are Bangladesh, Brazil, China, Germany, India, Indonesia, Japan, Mexico, Nigeria, Pakistan and Russia.

[2] U.S. Census Bureau, *Statistical Abstract of the United States, 2000*; Washington, D.C.; table 53.

[3] Source: "Forty-Three Percent of First Marriages Break Up Within 15 Years," Centers for Disease Control, May 24, 2001, published online.

[4] U.S. Census Bureau online, "Table A1: Marital Status of People 15 Years and Over, by Age, Sex, Personal Earnings, Race and Hispanic Origin/ March 2000," release date June 29, 2001.

[5] ibid

[6] U.S. Census Bureau online, table MS-1, Current Population Reports, Series P20-514.

[7] The Centers for Disease Control and Prevention issued a report, "First Marriage Dissolution, Divorce and Remarriage in the United States," in May 2001. The report indicated that one-fifth of marriages result in divorce within five years, one-third within 10 years, and 43% within 15 years.

[8] Barna Research Group, 2000-2001 survey data, N=7996.

[9] This perspective is perhaps best explained in Barbara Dafoe Whitehead's book, *The Divorce Culture* (Alfred Knopf: New York, 1997).

[10] U.S. Census Bureau, *Statistical Abstract of the United States, 2000*; Washington, D.C.; table 64.

[11] U.S. Census Bureau online, "Table A1: Marital Status of People 15 Years and Over, by Age, Sex, Personal Earnings, Race and Hispanic Origin/ March 2000," release date June 29, 2001.

[12] U.S. Census Bureau, *Statistical Abstract of the United States, 2000*; Washington, D.C.; table 55.

[13] U.S. Census Bureau, *Statistical Abstract of the United States, 2000*; Washington, D.C.; table 1213.

[14] U.S. Census Bureau, *Statistical Abstract of the United States, 2000*; Washington, D.C.; table 738-741.

[15] Ibid

Chapter 2
THE SELF-IDENTIFICATION OF SINGLES

Much of what you do – and don't do – in life flows from your perception of yourself. Our self-view is founded upon a complex and ever-changing mixture of ideas concerning our psychological composure, our emotional make-up, our economic standing, our core behavioral choices, and our relationship with God. Those perceptions can either free us to pursue our dreams or shackle us to a prison of self-imposed limitations. Often, people juggle a mixture of freeing and limiting self-views.

One of the most surprising outcomes from our research is the tremendous similarity of self-perceptions between single and married adults. This is partially because our marital status is just one of several perspectives we consider when developing our self-view. People categorize themselves in terms of their nationality, vocation, generation, faith affiliation, racial or ethnic orientation, sexual preference, affluence, ideological leanings, and many other factors. Marital status competes for supremacy or even conscious existence with a multitude of attributes.

Similar or dissimilar, though, to live, serve and work in harmony with single adults demands a solid comprehension of their understanding of self.

Psychological and Emotional Self-Perceptions

One of the most significant elements of our self-view pertains to our assessment of how we relate to people. Overall, we found that single adults view themselves as highly relational; they like to have control without instigating conflict, and are more likely to feel lonely or disconnected than are married individuals. When compared to married adults, singles are just as likely to deem themselves very relational and to desire control. They were notably more likely to eschew conflict, feel misunderstood by others, and to seek a handful of reliable friendships.

To get an accurate feel for these distinctions, though, we have to dissect the singles population into its component groups, for there are some important dissimilarities on these matters. For instance, singles who have never been married are more likely than any other adults, married or not, to be searching for a few good friends. About half of all never-been-marrieds are striving to develop additional relationships, which is considerably more common than the one-third of married adults who are also seeking to expand their extramarital relational ties. Presumably, one's spouse fills a substantial portion of the relational needs among married people. Divorced and widowed adults, while slightly more likely to be searching for meaningful relationships than are married adults, are also older and more established in their lifestyles and therefore may feel more deeply connected than their younger, never-been-married counterparts. In the interest of bonding with others, it appears that never-marrieds may minimize their involvement in conflict.

The fact that the relational self-perceptions of divorced and widowed adults more closely reflect those of the married contingent may also suggest that age and life experience are more important determinants of relationship capacity than is marital status.

However, the fact that never-been-married individuals are almost twice as likely to feel that they are often misunderstood by others, and that even the divorced and widowed are almost 50% more likely to feel that way than are married adults, suggests that the intimacy enjoyed through marriage goes a long way toward helping people feel that they get a fair hearing.

Singles and Their Relationships[1]

self-description	SGL	NBM	WID	DIV	MAR
avoid conflict whenever possible	76%	77%	81%	65%	65%
like to be in control	68	70	60	72	64
very relational	65	69	55	65	67
trying to find a few good friends	47	52	40	41	34
often misunderstood by others	43	46	38	37	27

(Key: SGL = all single adults; NBM = never been married; WID = widowed; DIV = divorced; MAR = married)

The data in the accompanying table point out that divorced people are slightly more likely than people from any other segment to enjoy control. Could this need for control have contributed to the split up of their marriage? Also notice that the widowed niche occupied one end of the continuum when it came to conflict (they're more likely to avoid it), control (they're less anxious to have it), and being very relational (they're lower in that dimension than any other segment). In other words, widowed adults, who are generally in their mid-sixties and beyond, want to "go along and get along" – they may perceive their future to be too short to squander it pursuing and battling with others.

More than nine out of every ten Americans, regardless of their marital state, think of themselves as self-sufficient. We're generally a skeptical lot, as well, although divorced adults lead the way in this regard. You can imagine that, having endured the dissolution of a critical relationship with someone they trusted and had invested in knowing, they are now less prone to accept claims made by people whom they know less well.

The Emotional State of Adults[2]

self-description	SGL	NBM	WID	DIV	MAR
self-sufficient	94%	92%	98%	95%	91%
skeptical	61	58	53	71	56
stressed out	35	37	27	33	29

(Key: SGL = all single adults; NBM = never been married; WID = widowed; DIV = divorced; MAR = married)

Oddly, the highest stress level is exhibited by never-been-married adults, with nearly four out of ten describing themselves as stressed out. Interviews revealed that such stress is often generated by either their relational activities or by their financial and career challenges – and, often, by both. Slightly fewer divorced individuals feel stressed out (one-third), while even fewer widowed and married people embrace such a description (one-quarter).

Economic Self-View

A fairly clear and strong correlation exists between financial security and one's marital status. In the table below, notice that married people are substantially more likely than singles, of any type, to state that they are financially comfortable and are generally less willing than singles to suggest that they are struggling financially. It seems that divorce takes a deep toll on one's financial stability: divorced adults were the only segment among which less than half said they were financially comfortable. While a substantial proportion of marriages dissolve at least in part due to financial tensions, the act of dismembering the marriage does not appear to alleviate the monetary difficulties that the partners experience.

Money and Marital Standing[3]

self-description	SGL	NBM	WID	DIV	MAR
financially comfortable	56%	60%	63%	47%	70%
personally struggling with finances	37	37	36	37	28
in debt	37	39	18	44	36

(Key: SGL = all single adults; NBM = never been married; WID = widowed; DIV = divorced; MAR = married)

The issue of personal debt is intriguing, as well. Nearly half of divorced adults, and about four out of ten married and never-been-married adults admit to being in debt. The widowed niche was least likely to adopt this self-view, with just one out of five embracing the label. But the types of debt faced differ for each group. Never-been-married adults face the costs of getting started in life: paying off college loans, car loans, and the acquisition of basic living needs (e.g., furniture, clothing suitable for work, etc.). Divorced adults struggle with debts incurred while married, alimony payments, and the costs associated with starting over again. Widowed adults feel least pinched because they are most likely to have their mortgages paid off, to have retirement and insurance benefits kicking in, and to have learned how to keep their spending under control. (The Bureau of Labor also informs us that a greater proportion of older people than ever before is remaining in the work force – generally in a part-time position, but nevertheless generating a small flow of revenue.) Many senior citizens also note that they have been preparing themselves for a change in lifestyle, getting ready to downgrade their spending to match their reduced income after they retire.

Perhaps the most important outgrowth of the research, however, is the insight that among never-been-married and divorced adults, finances feel like a veritable sword of Damocles waving dangerously above their heads, ready to fall upon them without notice. Not by accident, most married women, whether they have children or not, are employed: to maintain a desired standard of living, most couples feel they have no alternative but to have both partners bringing in revenue. One of the dangers this raises, of course, is converting marriage into an economically-driven arrangement, rather than a permanent bond based upon shared love, experience and vision.

Time, Energy and Focus

Americans are world-renowned for their frenetic pace of life, yet most of us feel we can handle it. With one notable exception, only about half of all adults feel their lives are too busy. That exception is the widowed population, among whom just one-quarter suggest that they are too busy.

Views on the centrality of one's career vary widely, though, based on life stage and marital status. Never-been-marrieds, who are typically in their twenties and thirties, are by far the most likely to be career-focused; nearly half say they fit the description: "career comes first in my life." In comparison, only one out of every ten married adults makes the same claim. Distracted by a plethora of other duties, many related to their marriage and children, married people are more likely to see their career as a means to an end, whereas never-been-marrieds tend to view their job (along with their personal relationships) as a defining reality. Divorced adults are caught in between these two views, with one-quarter admitting that their career is central in their life. Ample anecdotal evidence exists to support the notion that many marriages have failed because of the centrality of work for one or both spouses.

While our research did not dig deeply into the issue of addictions, a surprisingly large proportion of people admitted to struggling with an addiction of some type. Such obsessions were most common among those who have never been wed and those who are divorced. The fact that one out of five divorced adults cited an addiction in their life may again point to a key reason why their marriage broke up – or, in some cases, how they responded to the collapse of their marriage.

Defined By Activity[4]

self-description	SGL	NBM	WID	DIV	MAR
too busy	44%	47%	24%	53%	49%
career comes first	32	43	14	27	11
dealing with an addiction	13	13	5	18	8

(Key: SGL = all single adults; NBM = never been married; WID = widowed; DIV = divorced; MAR = married)

The attitudinal preferences listed in the table below illustrate how similar married and unmarried people are on many core perspectives – with the exception of widowed adults. Most people desire new experiences, especially among never-been-marrieds (essentially a generational thing) and least among the widowed. Nearly three-quarters of all adults also appreciated occasional deep discussions –even more so among widowed persons. However, adults generally like to keep things light. Infrequent heavy conversation enables them to maintain both their hectic pace of life and their ability to remain optimistic and hopeful.

Although a study we conducted a few years ago showed that most adults are optimistic about the future and their place in it, seven out of ten singles spend time regularly pondering their future. Widowed adults are somewhat less likely to do so, but even a majority of our widowed citizens often consider the long-term possibilities that lie before them in life. In addition, most adults also spend time fretting over the moral state of the nation. This issue is less frequently and less seriously considered by never-been-married people than by the other four niches we're exploring, but that is a function of both life cycle and generation.

Preferences That Show How We View Ourselves[5]

self-description	SGL	NBM	WID	DIV	MAR
like to try new experiences	79%	88%	59%	75%	76%
enjoy deep discussions	76	76	82	72	73
like to keep things light	74	71	80	74	72
concerned about the future	70	71	60	71	68
concerned about the moral condition of the U.S.	70	64	83	74	79
enjoy making tough decisions	52	53	49	50	52
searching for meaning and purpose	51	55	44	44	35
sociopolitical ideology:					
mostly conservative	23	19	33	24	37
mostly liberal	17	20	12	15	12

(Key: SGL = all single adults; NBM = never been married; WID = widowed; DIV = divorced; MAR = married)

About half of all adults say they enjoy making tough decisions. A similar proportion indicates they are actively seeking an understanding of the meaning and purpose of their life. For a matter that is so fundamental toward guiding daily choices and shaping values, that proportion is shockingly high. In fact, it's only marginally higher for teenagers than it is for adults, suggesting that most people make relatively little progress on this crucial insight. Faith and marriage are two factors that sometimes lead to an understanding of life purpose. Notice that married adults were somewhat less likely to still be searching for such answers, while the never-been-marrieds were the most likely to be deliberating on this matter. The two previously married segments – the divorced and widowed – reflect a type of crisis in this regard, with some individuals in those categories renewing their quest for purpose after their marriage has ended.

In terms of their sociopolitical views, most adults consider themselves to be moderate or middle-of-the-road in ideological matters. Again, this is a function of age and life stage more than marital status. One of the unexpected realities, though, is that young adults are more likely to embrace the "somewhere in-between" ground than to portray themselves as politically liberal or conservative. Deeper probing reveals that this is because they feel ill-informed on most issues and thus balk at taking a definitive stand; they are loathe to embrace labels, feeling that such categorizations are limiting, inaccurate and irrelevant. As members of a generation that is comfortable with contradictions they feel little kinship to either end of the ideological spectrum.

Divorce tends to move people more toward the political center, particularly away from the ideological right. The act of dissolving the relationship that they had counted on for stability, security and fulfillment raises numerous questions in the minds of divorced adults, facilitates a more profound sense of self-doubt and challenges their notions of how things work and what makes sense in life. One outgrowth of that self-doubt is a softening of their political views. Another consequence is a lessened likelihood of participating in the political process, including a diminished incidence of voting.

Religious and Spiritual Image

Over the past two decades Americans have become increasingly comfortable with and curious about spirituality. People's spiritual views and experiences play a central role in defining their nature and life.

Not surprisingly, four out of five adults consider themselves Christian. That label has become a generic term over the past quarter century, implying that someone is not associated with a non-Christian faith group rather than insinuating that they are a devoted follower of Jesus Christ.[6] Again, this self-perception is driven more by generation and life stage than by marital status. In the table below you will notice that the segment with the greatest accumulation of young people (i.e., never-been-marrieds) is twice as likely as older segments of the population to embrace the label "atheist" and is the least likely to adopt the label "Christian."

In like manner, spirituality is something that has greater appeal to older adults than to the youngest of adults. All of the talk about spirituality among young adults has confounded many cultural observers, leading them to posit that young adults are more spiritually inclined than are their elders. That turns out not to be the case, however. Young adults are divided into two camps: those who are deeply spiritual and those who

32

recognize the role of spirituality but have, at least for the time being, rejected or shelved it. Those who are spiritually-minded tend to be more intense in that focus than has been true among young adults in the past two decades, although they are also somewhat less likely to pursue Christianity as their sole faith of choice. At the same time, a surprisingly large proportion of the never-been-married group has rejected faith as a core life component and a viable means of self-description. Often, their distaste for religious experience and involvement stems from their sense that religious people and faith systems are either hypocritical or powerless. What is the driving force behind this conclusion? In many instances it is the divorce of their parents and of the parents of their closest friends – adults who had made faith a visible cornerstone in their life.[7]

Most people who delve into the spiritual realm consider themselves deeply immersed in it. (Again, the exceptions to the rule are the youngest adults.) This reflects the relative superficiality of American culture more than an intense affiliation with faith. Half of the never-been-married segment and nearly two-thirds of the married and divorced groups, and three-fourths of the widowed niche contend that they are "deeply spiritual." As we will see in Chapters 5, 6 and 7, this may be regarded as an overstatement of their spiritual commitment and depth. However, it is an important element to understand vis-à-vis how Americans see themselves. Most adults think of themselves as spiritual people. That self-image helps them to feel well-rounded, moral, and vertically as well as horizontally connected. In reality, the bulk of our population is more concerned about "touching base" with the spiritual dimension than with "owning" that dimension.

The Religious Self-Image of Americans[8]

self-description	SGL	NBM	WID	DIV	MAR
Christian	82%	78%	91%	85%	89%
spiritual	71	65	74	76	76
deeply spiritual	58	48	78	62	62
born again Christian	37	30	53	43	41
atheist	8	10	4	6	5

(Key: SGL = all single adults; NBM = never been married;
WID = widowed; DIV = divorced; MAR = married)

Another religious label that gets tossed about is "born again Christian." At this juncture in our journey into the lives of single adults we won't question the meaning of that term in the minds and hearts of those who embrace it. (We will explore this more deeply in Chapter 7.) Recognize, however, that despite the often-negative connotations associated with the label "born again Christian," three out of ten never-been-married, four out of ten divorced and married adults, and half of all widowed individuals adopt that term as an accurate self-description. The data also reveal that about half of widowed, divorced and married adults who view themselves as Christian also embrace the label "born again." This practice is less common within the never-been-married niche, among whom roughly two out of five self-professed Christians also think of themselves as being "born again."

(Let me also point out that elsewhere in this book when I use the term "born again" to describe a person, it is **not** based upon their self-identification as such. Barna Research uses a two-question approach to determining the likelihood of a person being born again. Our data reveal that only a weak correlation exists between people calling themselves born again Christians and actually having a relationship with Christ based upon

confession of sins and acceptance of His grace. We'll get into the details
of this in Chapter 7.)

A Wavy Mirror

A colleague in ministry with whom I shared the self-portrait painted
by single adults laughed in bemusement and asked, "Do you think that's
really how they see themselves? They are really self-deluded, aren't they?"
The answer to that question is not nearly as important as recognizing that
there may well be a substantial gap between how single adults see themselves and how married adults – like my friend – see them.

It is not uncommon to find that a person's self-view is not shared by
those who observe them from afar. For those who wish to effectively work
with single adults, whether that be as a friend, an employer, a family mem-
ber or a representative of Christ, our challenge is not to correct those
self-impressions but to understand them and work in tandem with those
perceptions. "Maybe the best we can hope to do," explained a counselor
to singles with whom I spoke, "is to hold up a mirror and help them see
themselves in the most objective light possible. I can't change them and
you can't change them – that's between themselves and God. Frankly,
since any changes that you or I would initiate are subjective, based on our
personal values and beliefs, changing them isn't a very hopeful enterprise,
and, sometimes, not a very healthy or beneficial venture for either party.
We'd be better off understanding who they think they are, helping them to
clarify and evaluate that self-image, and then working with them within the
boundaries of that perception."

Footnotes

[1] Based on a national survey of 1002 randomly selected adults; including 469 single adults, conducted by the Barna Research Group, January 2000.

[2] ibid

[3] Based on a national survey of 1005 randomly selected adults, including 504 singles, conducted by the Barna Research Group, January 2001.

[4] Based on a series of nationwide surveys among 6038 adults, including 2847 single adults, conducted by the Barna Research Group between January 2000 and November 2001.

[5] Based on a national survey of 1002 randomly selected adults, including 469 singles, conducted by the Barna Research Group, January 2000.

[6] For a deeper discussion of the spiritual condition of America, examine the research described in my recent book, *Growing True Disciples* (WaterBrook: Colorado Springs, 2001).

[7] These conclusions are drawn from studies we have been conducting among teenagers, in which we find young people whose parents divorce and whose closest friends' parents divorce are likely to shift from being comfortable with the Christian faith to being uncomfortable with all faith groups.

[8] Based on a national survey of 1005 randomly selected adults, including 504 singles, conducted by the Barna Research Group, January 2001.

Chapter 3
HOW SINGLE ADULTS LIVE

One overlooked joy of modern American life is watching diversity in daily choices and activities play out. While most of us take such freedom, independence and diversity for granted, the range of choices and sheer unpredictability of people's behaviors and preferences can be both frustrating and exciting. But rarely does such rampant individuality lead to boredom. The idiosyncratic lifestyles of single adults are a prime example of Americans doing what they do best: being themselves.

Most Americans, regardless of their marital status or age, believe that the greatest challenge in life is to achieve happiness and fulfillment. In fact, we discovered that most adults contend that God blesses them so that they may experience a heightened sense of enjoyment and personal fulfillment in life; only a relative handful understand the Genesis 12 principle that we are blessed so that we might be a blessing to others. Absent that servant-like perspective, most people focus on their personal goals, preferences and needs toward reaching happiness.

Happiness in Singledom

You might be surprised to learn that a large majority of single adults – 64% of the total, or roughly two-thirds – describe themselves as "extremely satisfied" or "very satisfied" with their life. You might be even more surprised to discover that this level of life satisfaction pales in comparison to that measured among married adults, almost nine out of ten (85%) of whom claim to be extremely or very satisfied with their life. Among single adults, widowed individuals have the highest levels of satisfaction (74%), trailed by the never-been-married niche (67%) and the divorced segment (55%).[1]

From these numbers, we can glean two insights. First, most single adults are pleased with the way their life is unfolding. Clearly, marriage is not required to live a fulfilling and pleasing life in America these days. Most single adults have figured out how to cope with the pressures and challenges of life with the help of family, friends and their own unique skills and abilities.

Second, single adults are likely to find that a healthy marriage will increase their joy in life. The quality of that marriage is important, however, as witnessed by the fact that barely half of divorced adults (55%) are greatly satisfied with their life. A strong marriage may alleviate some of the biggest challenges that single adults face, but a rocky union often results in a divorce and the numerous hardships that such dissolution produces, including a sense of isolation and personal failure.

Happiness is a composite perspective, though, based upon a combination of attitudes pertaining to core life dimensions. We discovered that single adults are most satisfied with their spiritual and emotional experiences, somewhat less at peace with their professional or occupational life, and least satisfied with their material and financial experience. Further insight is gleaned by recognizing that when their satisfaction levels are compared to those of married adults, the biggest gaps emerge in connection with their emotional and relational undertakings (15 percentage points less satisfied than married adults) and their financial state (13 percentage points lower).[2]

Checking Out the Checkbook

If it's true you can tell the priorities in a person's life by examining their checkbook, then the things that matter most to single adults are their home, their car and their stomach. Combined, those three elements consume three out of every five dollars they earn. Relatively small amounts – anywhere from 2% to 5% of their aggregate earnings – are devoted to clothing, health care, transportation, entertainment, education and contributions. Taxes consume nearly one-tenth of their income.[3]

Widowed adults allocate their incomes quite differently from other singles. These individuals – mostly elderly women – devote nearly half of their income to housing expenses. Health care, food and transportation each require an average of 13% of their earnings. Health care takes a deep bite out of their funds, consuming two-and-a-half times the percentage of their annual revenue as spent on health care by other single adults. Widowed adults eat a greater number of their meals at home than do other singles; never-been-marrieds and divorced people nearly split their meal money between home and eating out. Widowed adults also give away more money each year than does the typical never-been-married or divorced individual – even though the younger singles earn considerably more than do widowed folk, on average. The significance of this commitment is underscored by the fact that the typical widowed adult dips into his or her savings each year, draining nearly a thousand dollars from their reserve to get by. In that light, their generosity is especially commendable.

The significant differences in priorities between married and single adults relate to housing, transportation and giving. Married individuals pay a smaller share of their total income for housing – only about one-quarter, compared to about one-third among singles. Married people allocate more money for transportation but give away only half as much of their income as singles donate to churches and other non-profit organizations. In fact, the average widowed adult donates three times the share of his or her income to causes that married adults contribute. Relatively few single adults are wealthy, but they tend to donate a greater slice of their pie to those in need than do married couples.

Eating Is Not About Food

The eating habits of most single adults leave a lot to be desired. Nutritionists claim that most singles – particularly the young, active, never-been-married group – make a habit of eating unbalanced meals. A recent Roper survey showed that only one in four single adults actually eats three meals a day; the norm is one or two meals, supplemented by a series of snacks throughout the day. While that regimen is not necessarily harmful, the removal of home economics and life skills classes from school curricula in recent years has left most single adults without cooking skills, producing a nation of unmarried fast-food addicts. Research into consumer shopping patterns confirms that the days of cooking "from scratch" are long gone; convenience, speed and ease are the holy trinity of food preparation these days. Since singles spend less than a half hour in the grocery store on an average visit – and grocery shopping is way down on the list of favorite things to do – the popularity of fast-cook and pre-cooked meals has risen on a curve that parallels the growth of the single adult population.

For many singles, eating is not about nutrition or the joy of cooking: it's about survival and relationships. Whenever possible, many single adults use meals as an opportunity to spend time with friends. The restaurant industry over the past few years has buzzed about the latest trend, known as "dash-board dining," in which a small group of friends cram themselves into a car, head to the nearest fast-food joint, and eat in the car while carrying on a riveting conversation. Believe it or not, this has become the third most popular type of eating experience among singles, trailing only making a home-cooked meal and eating a convenience meal at home. As we will discuss, the factors that make this work are the provision of a novel or comforting experience and the ability to maintain and deepen relationships – two top priorities in the lives of singles.

Entertain Me

Even more than most Americans, single adults love to be entertained. One of the hallmarks of our culture in the initial decade of the twenty-first century is our addiction to experiences and adventures. Increasingly, we are adopting the post-modern notion that we work primarily to earn enough money to afford to play more frquently and more enjoyably. More than ever, we judge the value of relationships and organizations on the basis of the experiences they facilitate in our lives. Nowhere is this more evident than when we explore the lifestyles of single adults.

41

You can see it in their spending. Americans spend roughly the same percentage of their income (approximately 5%) on entertainment, regardless of their marital status. The areas in which singles spend more money than do married adults, in percentage terms, include reading materials, consumer electronics (excluding computers), entertainment events (largely music, sports and movies), and meals and drinks. Among the areas in which they spend less are computer software and accessories, outdoor activities and equipment, and magazines.

Reading is not a major entertainment form for young singles, but becomes a dominant practice among the oldest singles, particularly widowed adults. Overall, singles are responsible for about one out of every five books purchased each year in America, spending an average of about $125 annually on books. Married and widowed adults are more likely to read for pleasure during a typical week than are younger singles (especially the never-been-married niche). The latter segment tends to read for educational or vocational reasons to a greater extent, as they are seeking to get ahead in their career and to generate a more comfortable living. For many young singles, reading is seen as an appropriate endeavor for retired people, but not an activity for which they feel they can spare the time.

To a large extent, young singles substitute movies and videos for recreational reading. Although they convince themselves that time is not available for reading, most singles perceive the hours spent watching movies and videos to be a wise entertainment investment. The typical never-been-married individual sees nearly one new movie per month at theatres, and rents one or two additional movies per month. Older singles – especially widowed females – are less avid movie buffs, visiting theatres only a handful of times during the course of the year. Among single adults, one-quarter never go to the theatre.[4]

Listening to music is a major pastime for most single adults. Between radio, music videos and listening to compact discs and audiocassettes, singles spend more time listening to music than on any activity other than sleeping, working, and watching television. Once again, though, a huge gap stands between the listening habits of never-been-marrieds, divorced and widowed adults. The devoted music lovers are the younger brood – the never-been-marrieds. More than three-quarters of that segment buys recorded music during the year, compared to six out of ten divorced adults and just three out of ten widowed adults. The types of music they buy vary considerably, as well. Whereas never-been-married individuals are most likely to purchase rock, rap and R&B recordings, divorced adults most often select rock or country music, while widowed adults prefer Christian and country.

These purchases reflect the divergent musical tastes of each group. The table below allows us to compare the relative favorability of the major genres of music in the eyes of each singles niche. Among the never-been-married contingent, the genres that have more supporters than critics include R&B, pop, Christian, jazz and alternative rock. A greater proportion of these adults dislike rap and country than enjoy them, while rock music gets a mixed rating (although most of the disapproval relates to heavy metal). Among widowed adults, the favored styles of music include Christian, country and classical, while their least enjoyed sounds include rap and rock (especially heavy metal). Divorced adults are the most eclectic group, leaning towards pop, Christian, country, R&B and jazz, while strenuously rejecting rap and also turning their backs on rock. To put this in context, married adults are most enamored of Christian, classical and country music while a majority chose rap as their least favorite genre, distantly followed by rock.

Favored and Disliked Musical Styles of Singles and Marrieds[5]

	favorite style of music				most disliked music style			
	NBM	WID	DIV	MAR	NBM	WID	DIV	MAR
rock	18%	8%	17%	18%	20%	27%	28%	32%
R&B	16	*	5	3	2	*	*	1
rap/hip hop	9	*	1	1	25	35	46	52
pop	8	3	4	7	3	3	*	3
X	8	24	11	16	2	1	*	1
country	6	20	18	14	22	8	10	9
jazz	6	5	9	3	*	7	*	2
dance/swing	4	4	3	2	2	1	2	1
alternative	4	*	1	*	*	*	*	*
classical	3	12	7	9	2	*	3	1
Latin	3	*	4	2	1	*	*	*

(Notes: most disliked form of music – rock includes "heavy metal")
 : * indicates less than one-half of one percent)
Key: NBM = never-been-married; WID = widowed; DIV = divorced; MAR = married)

Inform Me

Single adults have varied levels of interest in current affairs, but a general pattern is evident: the older the person, the more likely they are to pay attention to news.

Across-the-board, singles most often rely upon network TV news, local TV news, daily newspapers and cable news networks. But the relative importance of various information sources varies from singles niche to singles niche. Never-been-married individuals are more likely than their unmarried counterparts to turn to MTV, the Internet, and morning TV magazine shows, and less likely than others to use newspapers, Sunday morning commentary programs on TV, and religious radio programs for insight. Widowed adults are more prone to seek news from local TV news and less enamored of cable network news, MTV, late night TV programs, and the Internet. Divorced adults are more likely than others to glean insights from network TV news, weekly national news magazines, the daily newspaper, public TV, and religious radio. They are less prone to consider sources such as MTV and the Internet.

In terms of raw appetite for news stories, the widowed population wins, hands down, while never-been-married and divorced adults are generally somewhat indifferent to the goings-on around the world. Single parents, in particular, make little effort to stay abreast of world affairs, largely due to the busyness of their days. In fact, the ability to catch up on the news without making major personal sacrifices is often a sign that indicates they have passed from the overloaded single-parent stage to the empty nest single-parent phase.

Friends and Family

For most singles adults, friends and extended family are central to their existence. For never-been-married adults, the tribal relationships exemplified in television shows such as *Friends* are common. Group activities remain popular, reducing the pressure on each individual to consistently facilitate compelling outings. Dating is widely viewed with trepidation, partially because the stakes are perceived to be high: finding a "soul mate" is no simple task, and the process of dating is deemed to be alternatively expensive, awkward or frustrating. The housing situation for many never-been-marrieds is also surprising: one out of every five 25 to 29-year old and one out of ten 30 to 34-year old men, as well as one out of twelve women in the 25 to 29 age category are still living at home with their parents. While this facilitates close ties with their aging parents, it also raises relational challenges unforeseen by most parents.

Divorced adults devote most of their relational time to interacting with their children and with their colleagues from work. Plunging into the dating zone is especially awkward for many divorced people. Although most of them eventually get remarried, a pattern follows the divorce: after an average of eight years of marriage and then the divorce, they spend two to three years being conspicuously "out of the market," another two to three years dating, a year or two seriously dating a prospective mate, then they remarry. Most of these people speak of competing tensions as they strive to regain stability in their life. They struggle with the trauma of their shattered marriage, the heartbreak of interacting with their children differently, the challenge of redefining themselves, the difficulty of thinking about dating again, the emotional highs and lows that accompany dating, the ecstasy of finding a potential mate, the self-doubts that plague their planning for the next phase of their life, etc.

Millions of divorced adults struggle to find equilibrium in their reshaped relationship with their children. The parent who gains custody of the children must usually juggle childrearing duties with sole-breadwinner status. The parent who loses custody must adjust to the occasional, scheduled visit. In four out of five cases, single-parent moms are awarded primary custody of the kids, but in half of those households, the family lives in or on the brink of poverty. These parents are much more intentional than many married parents about the time they spend with their kids.

Widowed adults divide their time between extended family and peers they meet through the organizations with which they associate (e.g., churches, clubs, seniors associations). Relatively few widowed folk emerge from their time of grieving with a determination to remarry. Since the 1960s large portions of the seniors segment has been moving into housing designed to meet their special needs and interests. Today, one-quarter of all senior citizens live in one of the nearly 30,000 assisted-living facilities throughout the country. Almost half of all elderly people will live in a nursing home, assisted care complex or other type of residential care option. It is in these places that seniors – and especially widowed seniors, most of whom are female – build many of the new and significant friendships.

On the lighter side of relationships, many single adults share their life with a pet, although singles surprisingly are less likely to have a pet than are married adults. (To understand why, think "kids.") In fact, married-couple households are two and one-half times more likely to own a dog, twice as likely to have a cat, and twice as likely to own a bird as are single adults. Widowed adults are more likely to own household pets than are other singles, but even their rates of pet ownership are lower than those of family households.[6] Most single adults regard pets as another point of responsibility rather than a source of companionship.

Singles and Sex

In a society as fascinated with sex as ours, it is not surprising to learn that the absence of marriage has failed to stop most single adults under the age of 50 from having regular sexual interludes. This practice is encouraged by contemporary marketing (promoted by the "sex sells" philosophy of Madison Avenue), the rise of the postmodern worldview ("there is no right or wrong, only you can decide what's right and appropriate for you"), and the mixed messages people receive while growing up (ranging from "what you do with your body is completely up to you" to "practice safe sex" to "abstain from all sex until you are married").

The consequence of our sexual obsession and lack of moral absolutes is that among 21-year olds, less than one out of five are married, but more than four out of five have had sexual intercourse – and most of them have had sex with multiple partners by that age. There are a number of implications of this state of affairs. First, few people getting married for the first time are virgins prior to marriage. Sexual activity continues long past the teen years for most single women: 42% of single women under 45 years of age have sexual intercourse during a typical year.[7]

Second, such rampant sexual experimentation has led to America performing more abortions than any other nation in the world. Thankfully, the number of known abortions has declined somewhat since the mid-90s, yet we continue to sustain more than 25 abortions for every 100 live births that take place. Among women under 25, the ratio is much higher, at more than 40 abortions for every 100 live births.[8] Eighty-percent of all abortions are performed on single women.[9]

Third, the U.S. has the world's highest rate of pregnancies among unmarried teenagers and among unmarried women. More than one million babies are born annually to unmarried women – one-third of the total live births in our country. This is most common in the black community, where two out of every three births are to a single mother. Among Hispanic women, two out of five births are to unwed mothers.[10] The Census Bureau notes that births outside of marriage continue to escalate, while the National Center for Health Statistics points out that births to unmarried women are most common among females 18 to 24-years of age. Although a large proportion of the children born to unwed mothers are "not wanted," of those who are born just 2% are placed for adoption, and those raised by their birth mother have a higher incidence of child abuse, health crises, behavioral problems, substance abuse and academic underperformance.[11]

A final consequence worth noting is that the Centers for Disease Control report that 65 million Americans carry an incurable, sexually transmitted disease (STD), and that an additional 15 million people are infected with such a disease each year. In total, they estimate that one out of every four teenagers already has an STD.

While the movement toward sexual abstinence in the past half-decade has borne some positive fruit, the big picture shows that most single adults, even if they get through high school and the college years with their virginity intact, generally fall prey to sexual temptation once they enter the "real world." Like any addiction, the research reveals that once adults have sexual intercourse with someone, that behavior continues.

Mothers At Work

Government statistics indicate that a majority of mothers are now employed outside the home, at least part-time. As difficult as life is for the typical working mother, you can imagine how challenging and exhausting it is to be a single mom, one of the eight million women who simultaneously serve as solo parent, chief breadwinner, head of the household and friend to others. Hard as they try to keep it all together, most single moms admit that they feel as if they are fighting a losing battle. If economics is any indication, there is some factual basis to support their feelings. The median annual income for single mothers is barely $25,000 – a solid 35% below the national household average. Among minority single moms, the picture is even worse, averaging less than $20,000 annually, resulting in a majority of minority children with unmarried mothers being raised below the poverty line.[12] This explains why more than four out of five married-couple families own their home, but a majority of single moms rent their residence.[13]

Single-parent women struggle to balance the multiple interests competing for their time and attention – not the least of which are their children. Exacerbating the challenge is the ever-escalating cost of raising a child these days. Estimates vary, but it is generally expected that raising a child born in 2000 through his or her 17th birthday will cost in the neighborhood of $165,000. For single-parent mothers who are awarded alimony, the average award is barely $3000 – and less than two-thirds of the designated recipients actually receive those payments. Despite the good intentions of the judicial system, holding down at least one full-time job is a "must do" activity for single moms.

According to a single woman's life stage, work carries a variety of connotations. Among the never-been-married women, their jobs play a significant role in shaping their identity, buttressing their self-worth, securing their independence, and facilitating new relationships with people who will become lifelong friends and possibly a spouse. Single mothers of pre-teens, most of whom are in their twenties and thirties, consider their job to be a means to an end – i.e., a source of income enabling them to raise their children. For some of these mothers, work is also an escape from the runny noses and whining about homework that causes their seemingly permanent headaches. For older women, especially widowed females, holding down jobs are less about economics and more about adding value and staying connected.

In the interests of fairness, single-parent dads have a tough time of things, too. Although there are fewer single-parent fathers with kids under 18 in their home – roughly two million – they face many of the same struggles as their female counterparts. The one comparative advantage they have is financial. The median income of these fathers is almost $40,000 – above the national household average. Minority single-parent fathers have a substantially lower median income than do white single dads (in the $30,000 to $33,000 range, depending on the ethnic group), but they fare much better than single-parent moms – even better than white single moms.[14]

Integrating Technology

Increasingly, technology is central in the lifestyles of single adults. The typical household is now equipped with many of the recent technological advances, from microwave ovens (which are used by most never-been-married adults on a daily basis, but are used by single moms less than any other segment of married or single adults) to cell phones and DVD players.[15] Most single adults rely upon these new products to save them time because time remains the primary obstacle that singles struggle to master.

Married-couple households are more likely than single-adult households to own most of the electronic technologies available today. This is not surprising given the spending levels of the diverse households on such equipment. While single adults tend to budget a higher percentage of their annual income for such devices (1.7% versus 1.3%, respectively), their smaller revenue base frees up less total dollars for such purchases, thereby limiting the immediacy with which they can acquire new appliances. The $415 spent, on average, by singles to get their hands on the latest communications and entertainment equipment (excluding computers) is considerably lower than the $700 that married-couple households invest in similar products each year.[16]

VCRs have become one of the most universally owned pieces of household equipment, rivaling television sets in their ubiquity. Never-been-married adults, however, have led the way in adopting DVD players, perceiving that these new units will be the wave of the future and thus constitute a wiser investment of their limited household funds. Cell phones have become a necessary appendage, particularly among the highly relational never-been-married set. (Divorced and widowed adults have been slower to see the value and to make the investment in cell phones.) Most singles have access to the Internet, although home-based access is more common among never-been-marrieds than the divorced, and twice as common as among the widowed. The general pattern, then, is that never-been-marrieds singles tend to sacrifice a bigger percentage of their income to have the latest and greatest technology, while divorced adults wait a while until prices come down and the technology becomes indispensable. Widowed adults typically remain impervious to the new developments, embracing them years after they have become common-place in most homes. Many widowed adults maintain that they have lived a long and satisfying life without the new contraptions and believe they can continue to live a fulfilling existence without such machines.

Household Electronic Equipment Owned[17]

equipment	SGL	NBM	WID	DIV	MAR
VCR	91%	93%	78%	94%	96%
cable TV	74	79	69	70	72
cellular telephone	53	59	48	48	61
desktop computer	48	52	34	50	63
CD-ROM player in computer	45	51	26	51	60
Net access on home computer	43	50	23	44	57
Net access on non-home computer	34	42	12	33	43
DVD player	19	23	16	15	18
satellite dish for TV	17	18	15	17	21
laptop/notebook computer	14	19	2	14	18
palmtop computer	5	9	5	0	10

(Key: SGL = single; NBM = never-been-married; WID = widowed; DIV = divorced; MAR = married.)

The Internet

The Internet has taken the world by storm over the past decade, changing our lives more than any technology since the development of the television. As noted above, accessing the Internet is a familiar, if not integral activity for most singles, with the exception of widowed adults. Overall, two-thirds of all single adults have access to the Internet either at home or at work. Access peaks among the never-been-marrieds (seven out of ten), followed by the divorced (six out of ten) and trailed by the widowed (just less than four out of ten). For context, realize that three out of four married adults have Internet access, a rate slightly higher than is true for the most connected singles niche.

Having access and using the Internet are two different elements, but the distinction is not significant in practical terms. Most people who have access to the Internet take advantage of that potential. Our research shows that among single adults, about half use the Internet at least once a week, about one out of ten use the Net on a less frequent basis, and nearly four out of ten never use the Net (which is almost exclusively the individuals who lack access). Never-been-marrieds are the most likely weekly users (two-thirds of them log on at least once a week), compared to about half of all divorced adults and only one out of eight widowed individuals. In total, three-quarters of widowed people never go online; in fact, only one-third of those who have access bother to surf the information superhighway.

The most interesting insight into Internet usage relates to the functions that people turn to the Net to fulfill. The accompanying table indicates that across-the-board, people's most common use of the Internet is to locate specific information. Slightly more than four out of ten single adults (and a slight majority of married people) rely upon the Internet to help maintain existing relationships and to buy products. Half of all never-been-married adults, three out of ten divorced adults, and one-quarter of married people use the Net to examine new videos or to listen to music. Among the least common uses of the Internet by single are to play video games (common among teenagers, but not among adults); participate in chat room discussions (one-fourth of the never-been-marrieds engage in such activity, compared to one in ten divorced and married people); make new friends (again, substantially more common among teens, but undertaken by only one-sixth of singles); and to have a religious or spiritual experience (one out of ten single adults do so). Interestingly, divorced adults are twice as likely to use the Internet for religious purposes as are married adults – often because these individuals feel ostracized or unwelcome at churches as a result of their divorce.

How Single and Married Adults Use the Internet[18]

use of the Internet	SGL	NBM	DIV	MAR
find information	96%	97%	96%	96%
maintain existing relationships	43	44	47	55
buy products	43	41	46	54
check new music, videos	43	50	30	26
play video games	27	28	26	18
chat rooms	22	28	11	11
make new friends	17	20	12	8
have spiritual/religious experience	10	9	12	6

(Key: SGL = single; NBM = never-been-married; DIV = divorced; MAR = married.)

Lifestyles Vary

One of the interesting observations from this review of single-adult lifestyles is that so much of what singles do relates directly to what they experienced growing up. The media they prefer, their sexual practices and values, personal spending habits, preferred music styles – all of these things and more become somewhat predictable by knowing a person's age and marital state. Be encouraged: it is quite possible to observe and understand these patterns and to convert that knowledge into sensitive and meaningful interaction.

Footnotes

[1] This is based on a national survey by the Barna Research Group, July 2001, among 1002 adults, including 496 single adults.

[2] These findings are from a national survey by California Survey Research, reported in USA Today, page D-1, February 9, 1999.

[3] Household spending figures in this section are based on several sources, but primarily upon the Consumer Expenditure Survey conducted annually by the Bureau of Labor Statistics. The most recent report available is for 1999, accessible from the Bureau's website.

[4] "Coming Soon," Pamela Paul, American Demographics, page 30, August 2001.

[5] Based on a survey by the Barna Research Group among 1005 adults, conducted November 2000.

[6] These figures are based on a variety of government studies reported in the Census Bureau's *Statistical Abstract of the United States – 2000*, (Washington, D.C.), 2000; tables 418-427.

[7] Census Bureau, *Statistical Abstract of the United States – 2000*, (Washington, D.C.), 2000; tables 55, 96, 97.

[8] Centers for Disease Control, *Health, United States 2001*, Washington, D.C., table 16, page 148.

[9] Census Bureau, *Statistical Abstract of the United States – 2000*, (Washington, D.C.), 2000; tables 103, 113.

[10] Census Bureau, *Statistical Abstract of the United States – 2000*, (Washington, D.C.), 2000; table 78.

[11] *Washington Watch*, December 2000, page 8.

[12] Census Bureau, *Statistical Abstract of the United States – 2000*, (Washington, D.C.), 2000; tables 738, 741.

[13] Census Bureau, *Statistical Abstract of the United States – 2000*, (Washington, D.C.), 2000; table 1213.

[14] Census Bureau, *Statistical Abstract of the United States – 2000*, (Washington, D.C.), 2000; tables 738, 741.

[15] The use of microwave ovens, other food preparation devices and household eating habits is described in a study by Peter Hart Research, as reported in *Advertising Age*, August 24, 1998, page 35.

[16] Based upon data from the Consumer Expenditure Survey conducted annually by the Bureau of Labor Statistics, 1999, www.bls.gov.

[17] Based on a survey by the Barna Research Group among 1005 adults, conducted January 2000.

[18] Data used by permission of The Barna Institute, from its report entitled "The Cyberchurch," released January 2001, available from www.barna.org. The study explores the relationship of technology and faith, and likely developments in this regard in the future.

Chapter 4
HEART STUFF:
GOALS, VALUES, MORALS
AND CORE ATTITUDES

A singles pastor recently told me, "Singles are just people. What's important about them isn't whether they have a husband or wife, but what they think is important in life, and how they pursue those things. All the talk about singleness is less important than diving beneath the surface and penetrating their hearts to perceive what motivates them. The last thing I want to hear about is the kind of person they want to marry – or avoid marrying again. What gets me involved in their life is understanding what they treasure, who they want to be and how they see themselves fitting into the world. I can't help them find a mate or find comfort in being single, but I can help them become all that God intended them to be – and that's fun!"

Single adults are merely people who are striving to understand themselves, their God, their world, and their place in God's world. The best route to empowering them to maximize their potential on this planet is to comprehend the "heart stuff" – their values, morals, goals and core attitudes. As much as anything, these elements define who they are, how they live, and where they are going in life.

The Role of Truth

Knowing a person's heart requires an exploration of their foundational perspectives on what is right and wrong, what matters most, and the source of wisdom in decision-making. These elements combine to forge a person's worldview. The most significant element of every person's worldview – and thus, the cornerstone of their decision-making process – is their perspective on moral truth. Even though most Americans call themselves "Christian," very few believe that that there is absolute moral truth conveyed by God through the Bible to direct our thinking and behavior. Most Americans – single or married, young or old, churchgoers or unchurched, born again or not – contend that truth is relative to the individual and his or her circumstances. The consequence of such thinking is the condition in which we find America today: moral anarchy and chaos.

A majority of Americans are clearly confused about such matters – and spend little time disentangling their thoughts on the issues involved. For instance, we find that half of all never-been-marrieds say they have no idea whether there is absolute moral truth or not, while two-thirds of those who have a position believe there are no moral absolutes. The picture is quite different among all single adults who have marriage experience (i.e., separated, divorced and widowed adults). Less than one-third do not have a position on moral truth, and those who have a perspective are more likely to argue that there are moral absolutes that do not change. Follow-up questions confirmed that a large proportion of adults who claim one position or another are not firmly convinced that their view is accurate.

The Existence of Moral Absolutes[1]

moral truth perspective	SGL	NBM	WID	DIV	MAR
there are moral truths or principles that are absolute; they do not change according to the circumstances	31%	18%	45%	44%	45%
there are no moral truths or principles that are absolute; moral truth always depends upon the situation or circumstances	30	32	34	25	27
have not thought about it/have thought about it but don't know what to believe	39	50	22	31	29

(Key: SGL = all singles; NMB = never been married; WID = widowed; DIV = divorced; MAR = married)

However, approaching the matter of truth from a different angle provides an entirely different outcome. When asked to identify the basis on which they make moral and ethical choices from day to day, even among people who perceive their choices to be founded on absolute beliefs, some of the foundations themselves are changing and relative.

The Basis of People's Moral and Ethical Decisions[2]

basis of moral and ethical decisions	SGL	NBM	WID	DIV	MAR
do whatever feels right/comfortable in a given situation	28%	29%	23%	25%	21%
follow principles/standards based on the values your family taught you	15	13	11	21	19
do whatever produces the best/most beneficial outcome for you personally	12	16	10	7	5
do whatever will make people happy	10	8	12	7	7
follow principles/standards based on the Bible	10	7	14	11	22
follow principles/standards based on your feelings	7	5	4	11	7
follow principles/standards based on your religious or church teachings (but not specifically the Bible)	6	2	5	8	11
follow principles/standards based on your past observations and experience	6	6	7	10	6
do whatever your family and friends expect	4	4	6	1	3

(Key: SGL = all singles; NMB = never been married; WID = widowed; DIV = divorced; MAR = married)

Overall, about one out of every four single adults base their moral and ethical decisions on what feels right or feels most comfortable in a situation. Similarly, about one-eighth of singles – ranging from 7% of the divorced to 16% of the never-been-married – decide on the basis of personal benefits from the decision. One out of ten seek to avoid conflict with others, basing their choices on what will make others happy or placated.

Close to half of all single adults base their moral choices on set standards and principles, but the nature of those standards and principles varies considerably – as does the percentage of each singles niche that relies on such standards. In total, just one out of three never-been-marrieds turn to such standards, compared to two-fifths of widowed adults and three-fifths of divorced adults. (Two out of three married adults do so.)

Even more disparity emerges when identifying the content of those shaping principles. For instance, slightly less than one in ten never-been-married adults (9%) turn to the Bible, or teaching from their church or religious experiences. Twice as many widowed and divorced adults (19%) rely on faith-based guidance. Clearly, however, relatively few single adults turn to their faith to shape their moral and ethical choices. Feelings, social expectations and personal benefit are the driving forces behind the moral choices of most singles.

Realize that most unmarried people – or married individuals, for that matter – do not wrestle with issues of truth and morality. In fact, just one out of every five never-been-marrieds and two out of five previously-married singles, as well as currently married adults, contend that knowing about moral truth is very important. To most Americans, life is fast-paced, complex, challenging and ever-changing. Most Americans believe that it's important to simply do your best and then move on without obsessing over what's right and wrong (since most people aren't even sure such realities exist),and without wasting much time analyzing your choices. After all, there's too much to do to worry about the implications of past choices.

Ideology and Political Participation

Single adults are located at a different place on the ideological and philosophical continuum than are married people. First, individuals who have been married – whether they are currently married, divorced or widowed – are about 30% more likely to be registered to vote than are people who have never been married. (Whereas 17 out of every 20 people with marriage experience are registered voters, only 13 out of 20 never-been-marrieds fit the same mold.) This disparity is largely related to one's sense of responsibility: being younger, having fewer people who rely upon them, and possessing a greater sense of independence and friskiness in life, never-been-marrieds are less prone to follow social and political issues, to feel a sense of impact, and to take their personal responsibility in the democratic process as seriously as do older, more established Americans.[3]

Involvement in the political process differs, too. One-third of married adults are registered Democrats, but close to half of all single adults claim that affiliation; two-fifths of married people are registered Republicans, compared to only one-quarter of all singles. This orientation suggests that single adults are sufficiently in tune with political perspectives to recognize that the Democratic Party is portrayed as one more sensitive to the needs of the less affluent and less influential people groups – a self-view that singles of all types would embrace. The fact that divorced and widowed individuals are more prone to align with the Democratic Party underscores the awareness of formerly-married adults to the groups that most overtly proclaim an interest in advancing the cause of single adults.

The ideological differences of single and married adults are perhaps best illustrated by examining their philosophical self-descriptions, levels of voting participation, and candidate preferences. Never-been-married people are much more likely to associate with liberal ideology. As a group, they are evenly divided between describing themselves either "mostly liberal" or "mostly conservative" on social and political issues. Divorced adults definitely lean toward the "mostly conservative" label," while widowed and married people are three times more likely to describe themselves as conservative than liberal.

Voting turnout amplifies these same differences. In the 1998 national elections, in which a presidential race was not involved, the "more single" a person was, the lower was their likelihood of voting. Only 26% of never-been-marrieds voted, compared to 38% of divorced adults, 47% of widowed adults, and 50% of married voters.[4] Similarly, in the 2000 presidential election, the same pattern emerged: never-been-marrieds were the least likely voters, divorced adults were somewhat more likely to have cast a ballot, and widowed and married individuals were the most prolific voters.

The choice of candidates in the presidential election followed a completely different pattern. A majority of each of the single adult niches supported Democratic contender Al Gore, while a majority of married adults sided with Republican candidate George W. Bush. Oddly, the ideological leanings of each people group were a weak predictor of their candidate preference. Never-been-marrieds, who lean liberal, were marginally more likely to have voted for Gore rather than Bush. Divorced individuals were twice as likely to support Gore as Bush. Widowed adults, one of the more conservative segments, decisively swung toward Gore. Married adults were the only group among these to push Bush – and they did so by about a 3-to-2 margin.

So what do these confusing patterns teach us? Simply that single adults are not an easy group to understand – often because they do not understand (or accept) themselves and their present state of being. They are influenced by a variety of inputs, making it hard to derive a black-and-white picture of who they are, what they think and how they behave. As was noted earlier, increasing numbers of Americans are comfortable with contradictions – even when the paradox in question relates to their own behavior!

Bear in mind that age and life stage remain dominant influences on people's thinking and behavior. Never-been-marrieds, often young adults, thus possess some generational traits that influence much of their behavior. They are comfortable with contradictions, independent in their behavior, and unpredictable in their choices. They are inconsistently involved in causes, even those in which their views and behaviors would lead observers to expect them to be deeply invested. Divorced people are walking the balancing act between thinking and acting like a single-again person as opposed to a married adult. Widowed individuals remain, in their minds, married – it's simply that their spouse is no longer living with them. Yet, they have to behave like a single person in many ways, causing frequent cognitive dissonance and role confusion.

What We Value

The goals we set for ourselves are driven by a combination of factors such as age, life experiences, education, worldview, faith commitment, and life stage. Consequently, as we examine the life priorities and future dreams of single adults, there is tremendous variation in terms of their life direction.

As the figures in the accompanying table indicate, never-been-married adults are most focused on maintaining their health, having close friends, living with integrity, getting married for life, and having a comfortable lifestyle. Widowed people are focused on health, life's purpose, their relationship with God, spending time with family, and remaining single. Divorced individuals have fewer driving goals for their lives than their single counterparts. Health is a major issue for them, followed by having close friends, a clear life purpose, and a solid relationship with God.

Some of the uniqueness among these three singles populations becomes even clearer when you explore their secondary strata of goals. For the never-been-married group, achieving a clear sense of their life's purpose heads the second echelon of goals, followed by having a college degree, enjoying a satisfying sexual relationship with their partner, having a close relationship with God, and remaining close to family. Some of the outcomes that did not make the cut included being deeply committed to the Christian faith (only four out of ten see that as a worthy goal), having children (slightly less than half see this as very desirable), making a difference in the world and influencing people's lives, traveling extensively, owning the latest technology and achieving fame or public recognition.

Personal Goals[5]

life outcomes deemed "very desirable"	SGL	NBM	WID	DIV	MAR
experiencing good physical health	88%	84%	88%	96%	93%
having close personal friendships	75	76	66	77	75
living with a high degree of integrity	74	76	67	69	87
having a clear understanding of the meaning and purpose of your life	72	70	76	72	78
getting and staying married to the same partner for the duration of your life	70	78	72	53	88
having a comfortable lifestyle	67	73	59	59	57
having a close relationship with God	67	61	77	72	74
living close to family/relatives	61	57	76	57	60
having a satisfying sexual relationship with your marriage partner	55	64	40	50	69
being deeply committed to the Christian faith	49	39	68	54	58
having a college degree	49	64	38	29	35
having children	48	46	43	51	61
being knowledgeable about current events	46	42	52	43	52
making a difference in the world	44	43	47	42	49
being active in a church	40	34	60	39	45
having a high-paying job	38	46	17	39	22
influencing people's lives	35	39	30	26	39
traveling throughout the world	29	29	26	29	23
owning a large home	25	28	24	17	16
owning latest technology/electronics	11	11	2	16	7
achieving fame or public recognition	7	7	2	5	5

(Key: SGL = all singles; NMB = never been married; WID = widowed;
DIV = divorced; MAR = married)

Widowed folks have radically redefined what's important in life given their typically advanced age and life experience. Beyond their top-rated goals, as listed above, secondary goals include being deeply committed to Christianity, living with integrity, having good friends, being active in a church, living comfortably and staying up-to-date on world affairs. Among the items that are irrelevant to most widowed people are sex, education, influence, travel, and household gadgets.

The divorced niche has yet a different spin on what's meaningful for their life. The secondary goals that drive them include living with integrity and comfort, living close to family, a deep commitment to Christianity, and having a fulfilling sexual relationship with a marriage partner. About half of all divorced individuals apparently look forward to remarriage, while the other half expect to remain single for the duration of their lives. Outcomes that do not get divorced adults excited include further education, staying current on world affairs, being active in a church, having influence, world travel, owning the latest in consumer electronics, and achieving fame.

Several intriguing patterns emerge from these figures. One such outcome relates to people's prioritization of their faith. Notice that each of the groups studied rated a personal relationship with God to be more important than being active in a church. However, the relative importance of church involvement varied. Only about half of the never-been-marrieds and divorced adults who prioritize a relationship with God also plan to pursue an active church life. That was considerably lower than the six out of ten married adults and eight out of ten widowed adults who held the same conviction.

Another interesting insight is the relative loss of intensity that divorced adults seem to possess regarding their future. While at least six out of ten never-been-married, widowed, and married adults identified nine goals they deem very desirable, only five outcomes reached that level among divorced adults. The average percentage of adults who listed the seven highest ranked outcomes was also substantially lower among divorced adults than for any other group. The act of divorcing their spouse affects their personal expectations in major ways.

A final revelation of importance is the relative disinterest that the youngest singles, mostly comprised of those who have yet to marry, have in relation to faith development. Young people traditionally rate such items lower than do older adults, but the level of difference between the young and the old is becoming larger as time goes on. The fact that less than two out of five young adults desire to be deeply committed to the Christian faith, and that only one in three want to be active in a church, sends a significant signal to church leaders about what lies ahead for congregations over the coming two decades. This information fits the pattern we have recently identified among teenagers and adolescents, who also have an interest in spiritual matters but little interest in the organized church.[6]

The Ranking of People's Goals[7]

life outcomes deemed "very desirable"	NBM	WID	DIV	MAR
experiencing good physical health	1	1	1	1
having close personal friendships	3t	8	2	5
living with a high degree of integrity	3t	7	5	3
having a clear understanding of the meaning and purpose of your life	6	3t	3t	4
getting and staying married to the same partner for the duration of your life	2	5	9	2
having a comfortable lifestyle	5	10	6	11
having a close relationship with God	9	2	3t	6
living close to family/relatives	10	3t	7	9
having a satisfying sexual relationship with your marriage partner	7t	14	11	7
being deeply committed to the Christian faith	15	6	8	10
having a college degree	7t	15	16	15
having children	11t	13	10	8
being knowledgeable about current events	14	11	12	12
making a difference in the world	13	12	13	13
being active in a church	16	9	14t	14
having a high-paying job	11t	16	14t	16

(Key: NMB = never been married; WID = widowed;
DIV = divorced; MAR = married; t = tie)

The Values They Espouse and Live

Describing people's worldviews and values gives us a sense of what's important and compelling to them. The research provides us with additional insights into how single adults convert those perspectives on truth and righteousness into practical ideas and actions.

If there is any doubt that the moral condition of the nation is crumbling, a series of surveys dispels any such doubts. One such project, conducted among teenagers and college students by Peter Hart Research, found that 58% of teens and 52% of college students believe they have lower moral standards than do their parents, while only 15% of teenagers and 13% of college students say they possess higher moral standards than do their parents.[8] Certainly ample proof of the truth of their assessment exists. Even though morality gets a lot of media and pulpit attention across the country, and expressions of moral concern have risen dramatically in national polls during the past decade, only a mere one out of ten unmarried adults listed morality as the most important priority for our political leaders to tackle.[9]

Sexuality and the Single Life

You cannot understand Americans unless you penetrate the role of sex and sexuality in their life. Like a finely cut diamond, there are numerous facets to grasping such insight, some of which are easier to see and interpret than others.

Co-habitation plays a role in this examination. Presently, there is a huge gap between single adults and married adults on this issue. Three out of four never-been-married adults contend that co-habitation is morally acceptable, while a smaller majority of marriage-experienced singles (62% of divorced adults and 56% of widowed adults) and a large minority of married adults concurs.[10]

If actions speak louder than words, then consider this: three times as many single adults are co-habiting today as twenty years ago.[11] A majority of couples live together before getting married these days, a substantial increase from the 10% who did so in 1965. Sadly, while a majority of cohabiters do so in an effort to improve the chances of their potential union lasting the course of time, statistics show that cohabiters have a 48% greater chance of experiencing a divorce than do individuals who did not live together prior to marriage.[12] Cohabiters who eventually marry are also more likely to be victims of domestic violence, depression, dissatisfaction with life, shorter life spans, and sexual anxiety.[13] In spite of all of these facts, a growing majority of young people (six out of ten) believes that cohabitation is a good idea.[14]

Giving birth to children outside of marriage is not necessarily an accident of careless sexual activity. One recent survey reports that a majority of twenty-somethings contends that having a child without being married is "a worthwhile lifestyle" choice. Among cohabiters who have a child, the percentage who marry after the pregnancy has declined from 57% in 1987 to just 44% in 1997.[15] One-third of all births each year are to unmarried women, the highest proportion of live births to single parents among any developed nation in the world. While most unmarried people take medical precautions to avoid an unwanted pregnancy, the one precaution that most of them refuse to adopt is abstinence.

One of the dominant solutions to an unexpected or unwanted pregnancy is abortion. As noted earlier in the book, Americans have more than one million abortions every year. The Centers for Disease Control and the Alan Guttmacher Institute have been tracking abortions for years. Their information indicates that eight out of ten legal abortions

69

are performed on single women, and that two-thirds of all of these procedures are among never-been-married females. Six out of ten women who have an abortion are white; 53% are performed on women who have not yet reached their twenty-sixth birthday. The most common reasons for having a baby aborted are predictable but chilling. Three-fourths say that having the baby would interfere with work, school or other responsibilities; two-thirds say they cannot afford to raise a child; half do not want to be a single parent or have additional conflict with their partner. Abortion is almost always a decision of convenience rather than necessity; just fifteen thousand of the 1.25 million or more abortions each year are due to rape or incest.[16]

Despite being a high profile and controversial issue since the Supreme Court opened the door for legal abortions a quarter century ago, millions of Americans still flip-flop on this issue. Among never-been-marrieds, half describe themselves as pro-choice, four out of ten say they are pro-life, and one out of ten avoid such labels. About half support legal abortions either in most or all cases, while one-quarter say they should be permitted only in a few special situations and one in five want all abortions outlawed. Divorced adults are evenly divided between those who call themselves pro-life and pro-choice. Four out of ten prefer legalizing abortions in all or most situations; one-third favor severe limitations on abortions; and one-sixth want to make all abortions illegal. Just less than half of all widowed adults support legal abortions in all or most circumstances, while one-quarter favor limited legality and one-quarter support complete illegalization.

Views On Abortion[17]

perspective on legalizing abortion	SGL	NBM	WID	DIV	MAR
should be legal in all/most circumstances	51%	55%	44%	42%	37%
should be legal in only a few circumstances	28	25	28	36	36
should be illegal in all circumstances	19	18	24	17	23
moral acceptability of having an abortion:					
it is morally acceptable	44	50	39	35	34
it is morally unacceptable	48	45	51	51	55
self-description on abortion issues:					
consider self to be pro-choice	52	58	40	44	43
consider self to be pro-life	37	34	42	41	49

(Key: SGL = all singles; NMB = never been married; WID = widowed;
DIV = divorced; MAR = married)

Americans have a tendency to have a more rigid personal standard than they want reflected in the law of the land. That condition is evident regarding abortion. It appears that most adults, including singles, want the laws to provide people with more latitude than they, personally, would take advantage of. As for the moral appropriateness of abortion, half of the never-been-marrieds claim that it is morally acceptable, compared to just four out of ten widowed adults and one-third of the divorced niche. (Overall, one-third of married adults deem abortion to be morally acceptable.) Along the same lines, a small majority of single adults favored FDA approval of the controversial French "abortion pill," officially known as RU-486.[18]

One of the growing challenges in the area of sexuality is pornography. Pornography on the Internet has become a multi-billion dollar industry in the span of just a few years. Add the continuing revenues from other purveyors of such material and the porn industry emerges as a $10-billion-plus sector. Although millions of parents are anguished about the potential of their children viewing unsolicited pornographic material on the Internet or in their e-mail, or the ease with which their offspring can access such material online, most singles contend that it is morally acceptable for adults to view sexually explicit matter.

Movies are the pornography medium given the greatest leeway by adults. Only one-fifth of widowed adults portray movies that show explicit sex or nudity as morally acceptable. That figure doubles among married adults, while a slim majority of divorced people and two-thirds of never-been-marrieds suggest that such movies are morally acceptable. Pornographic magazines are slightly less permissible in the eyes of single people. Oddly, more widowed people feel porn magazines are acceptable than feel sexually-explicit movies are morally acceptable. Smaller proportions of married (one-third), divorced (just under half) and never-been-married adults (three out of five) deem skin magazines morally acceptable than hold such views regarding sexually-explicit movies.

Views On Pornography[19]

perspective on pornography	SGL	NBM	WID	DIV	MAR
watching a movie with explicit sex or nudity:					
- morally acceptable	56%	67%	21%	53%	45%
- not morally acceptable	41	31	74	43	51
reading a magazine with explicit sexual pictures or nudity:					
- morally acceptable	52	62	29	46	36
- not morally acceptable	46	37	68	52	61

(Key: SGL = all singles; NMB = never been married; WID = widowed;
DIV = divorced; MAR = married)

Harboring sexual thoughts or fantasies about someone other than a spouse bothers relatively few people. Widowed adults were the only segment of the four marital status groups examined among whom sexual fantasies were more likely to be considered morally unacceptable than morally acceptable – and even among them less than half said such thoughts were illegitimate. Three out of five divorced people and three-quarters of the never-been-married contingent felt that such fantasies were morally acceptable.

One of the most controversial public issues of the day is that of gay rights. The increasing number of people who believe that homosexuality is something that you are born with, rather than a conscious behavior that is a choice – slightly more than one-third of all single adults, but up from less than one in ten just a decade ago – indicates how soft people's attitudes on this issue are, and that further change in people's views on the matter is likely.

Homosexuality is an issue on which the generational divide is most evident. Two-thirds of never-been-married individuals say homosexuality is an acceptable alternative lifestyle – nearly double the proportion of widowed people who hold that view, and considerably more than the 44% of divorced people and 39% of married adults who concur. The gap is even wider regarding the legality of homosexual relations between consenting adults: seven out of ten never-been-marrieds want to sanction gay relationships, while just less than half of divorced and married adults and only one-third of widowed adults agree. Perhaps surprisingly, there is much less support for clergy performing marriage ceremonies for gay couples, or blessing those unions. Again, the never-been-married segment is most supportive of this notion, but less than half endorse the idea, while only one out of four other single and married adults favor such clergy involvement. Among divorced adults, the idea is rejected by a 2-to-1 margin, while widowed adults disapprove by a 3-to-1 margin.

Again, people were more likely to endorse legal permission for homosexual relationships than to define them as moral. Just four out of ten never-been-marrieds, one-fourth of divorced adults and one out of eight widowed people said a sexual relationship between two consenting people of the same gender is morally acceptable. (One out of four married adults took that side as well.)

Views On Homosexuality[20]

perspective on homosexuality	SGL	NBM	WID	DIV	MAR
homosexuality between consenting adults:					
- should be legal	58%	69%	35%	46%	44%
- should not be legal	33	25	47	41	46
homosexuality as an alternative lifestyle:					
- should be considered acceptable	54	63	35	44	39
- should not be considered acceptable	39	33	49	44	52
you are born homosexual	37	37	36	35	35
you become homosexual due to external factors	46	48	38	47	48
clergy should perform/bless gay marriages	37	45	22	27	26
clergy should not perform/bless gay marriages	53	48	67	60	67
a sexual relationship with a person of same sex:					
- morally acceptable	32	39	13	24	22
- not morally acceptable	66	59	88	74	75

(Key: SGL = all singles; NMB = never been married; WID = widowed;
DIV = divorced; MAR = married)

Marriage

On the issue of divorce, most Americans want marital dissolution to be more difficult. One national survey had support for making a divorce harder to obtain outpacing making it easier to do so by a 3-to-1 ratio. There are extenuating circumstances that some people would take into account, however, most notable being the presence of children in the family. About one-third of all adults believe that a couple that has an unsatisfying marriage should remain together simply for the sake of their children.[21] A study from the University of Chicago found that men are much more likely to engage in adultery than are women, but that most

Americans contend that they have never engaged in adultery.[22] Most alarming, though, is the finding in another study of unmarried 20-some-things that two-thirds of the males and about half of the women in that age bracket would have sex with someone they found attractive, even though they had no interest in marrying them; and half of the men and one-third of the women in that age group believe it's acceptable to have sex with someone they really like even if they had known the other person for just a brief time.[23]

Not quite one out of every four adults, regardless of their marital status, say that if a couple gets divorced for a reason other than adultery, they have committed a sin. Perhaps this sentiment is driven by the widespread notion that although divorce is undesirable, it is almost inevitable these days. If current trends hold true, a majority of newly-married couples are likely to get divorced, an outcome that will not surprise too many Americans. One-quarter of all singles and one-fifth of married people say divorce is likely, while another two-thirds believe a marriage has nothing better than a 50-50 chance of survival.

Thankfully, most people still acknowledge that an extramarital affair is morally untenable. More than nine out of ten singles submit that a married person having an affair with another married person, other than their spouse, is engaged in a morally unacceptable act. Three out of four never-married and widowed adults, and two-thirds of the divorced niche, con-tend that a married person having an affair with an unmarried person is also morally unacceptable. (The survey did not probe the matter, but one must wonder if the fact that many more divorced people find affairs with unmarried people morally permissible is because it was that very activity that destroyed their own marriage.) It is also noteworthy that married adults are much less likely to find an affair between a married and unmarried person morally legitimate.

Views On Adultery and Divorce[24]

perspective on adultery and divorce	SGL	NBM	WID	DIV	MAR
divorce, except in cases of adultery:					
- is a sin	24%	25%	22%	22%	28%
- is not a sin	69	70	67	67	61
a married person having an affair with a married person other than their spouse:					
- is morally acceptable	6	7	4	6	5
- is not morally acceptable	93	92	93	94	94
a married person having an affair with an unmarried person:					
- is morally acceptable	26	23	22	32	11
- is not morally acceptable	72	74	75	65	86

(Key: SGL = all singles; NMB = never been married; WID = widowed;
DIV = divorced; MAR = married)

Substance Abuse

One of the best indicators of Americans' struggle with the notion of morality is their view on alcohol abuse. Most people would contend that excessive drinking has the potential to turn ugly, but surprisingly few young people are prepared to cast drunkenness as a corrupt behavior. A slight majority of never-been-marrieds say that getting drunk is morally acceptable. Just one-tenth of widowed people and three out of ten divorced adults concur.

Drug abuse remains a hot issue in the U.S.; both single and married people harbor serious concerns about drug use. Nine out of ten adults believe the country has a serious drug abuse problem to address, and about half of all adults (single as well as married) say the drug problem is serious in their own neighborhoods. It may seem odd, then, to also learn that half of all adults argue that too many people are put in jail simply for possession of narcotics. This is partially explained, though, by the fact that single adults are twice as likely to say that drug use should be treated more as a disease than a criminal offense. (Married adults are evenly split on that score.)[25]

The recent debates about using marijuana for purposes other than medicinal treatments also raised some marked differences of opinion. Seven out of ten single adults believe doctors should be allowed to prescribe marijuana to their patients to be used for medicinal reasons. Singles are also evenly divided on whether or not to make possession of small amounts of marijuana used for recreational purposes a criminal offense. (A slight majority of married adults lean toward making possession of any amount illegal.)[26] Once again, many singles are willing to legalize behaviors that they perceive to be morally unacceptable. In this case, a little more than one-third of all never-been-marrieds believe non-medicinal marijuana use is morally acceptable, compared to one-quarter of the divorced and one-seventh of the widowed populations.[27]

Integrity

Integrity has been defined as "what you do when nobody is looking." If that's the case, sometimes we may wish to have eyes in the backs of our heads to protect ourselves from the consequences of the failed integrity of others.

A good example of the decline of moral integrity is the fact that six out of ten single adults say sometimes it is necessary to lie just to get by. Another might be the reality of just one out of ten singles saying it is morally acceptable to cheat on income tax filings, yet discovering that two out of ten admit to having done so in the past. And how about the discovery that one-quarter of all never-been-marrieds say it is morally acceptable to knowingly keep excess change you receive by mistake at a store. (Just one out of ten widowed adults and one out of twenty divorced people hold the same view.) One out of seven widowed adults and one out of eight never-married people say that lying on a resume, if it will improve your chances of getting a job, is morally acceptable.[28]

Among the most clear-cut departures from traditional moral perspectives come in relation to never-been-marrieds concerning profanity and speeding. In both cases, a majority of these predominantly young people call intentionally breaking the speed limit while driving and the use of profane language morally acceptable behaviors. Again, this is generational rather than marital in genesis. One-quarter of widowed and divorced adults view profanity as morally defensible, while four out of ten divorced folks and only 15% of the widowed niche argue that speeding is moral behavior.[29]

Sometimes It Makes No Sense...

These perspectives provide an insider's glimpse into what makes unmarried people tick. In some cases, they are no different than married people, sometimes because their behaviors are influenced more by life stage or generation than by their marital state. In other cases they are radically different in their views and actions.

It also bears noting that the moral sensibilities of a substantial number of single adults seem rather warped. For instance, four times as many widowed adults are likely to say abortion is morally acceptable as are likely to portray getting drunk in the same manner. Divorced adults are more likely to condone pornography, homosexuality and cohabitation to getting drunk. The never-been-married folks in our nation are more prone to endorse pornography, cohabitation, abortion and homosexuality than to support getting blitzed or keeping excess pocket change from a grocery store. The reason is simple: lacking any moral standard as a basis for such considerations, the final determination of right and wrong is personal and conditional. The result is an unusual and unpredictable scrabble of values and behaviors.

Footnotes

[1] The data regarding morality is from a study by the Barna Research Group conducted in May 2001 based on a national sampling of 1005 adults interviewed by telephone. Additional analysis of the data is available in the Barna Update report released September 10, 2001, entitled "*Practical Outcomes Replace Biblical Principles As the Moral Standard,*" accessible via the Barna Research website at www.barna.org. A video presentation of George Barna describing the study is also available and can be acquired through the website.

[2] Based on a national survey of 2011 randomly selected adults, conducted by the Barna Research Group, July through November 2001. The survey included 970 single adults: 543 never-been-married people, 159 widowed adults, and 238 who are currently divorced.

[3] The data pertaining to political ideology and voting patterns in this portion of the chapter are drawn from a series of nationwide surveys conducted by the Barna Research Group among single adults between January 2000 and November 2001.

[4] Jennifer Day and Avalaura Gaither, *Voting and Registration in the Election of November 1998*, Current Population Report, August 2000, U.S. Census Bureau, Washington, D.C.; table C.

[5] Based on a survey of 1005 randomly selected adults, conducted by the Barna Research Group, January 2000. This survey included 469 single adults, 244 of whom had never been married, 83 of who were widowed, and 123 of whom were currently divorced.

[6] A more extensive discussion of this trend is included in my book *Real Teens* (Regal Books: Ventura, CA, 2001), which notes the misleading nature of the current high level of church involvement among teenagers and what we might expect in the future.

[7] These rankings are based on the data shown in the previous table, which is based upon a national survey of 1005 randomly selected adults, conducted by the Barna Research Group, January 2000.

[8] This study was conducted in September 1998 and reported in *Rolling Stone*, November 12, 1998, pages 79-80.

[9] Based upon a national survey conducted by the Pew Research Center in September 2000.

[10] Based on a national survey of adults by the Barna Research Group, conducted in May 2001 among 1003 adults.

[11] *Statistical Abstract of the United States – 2000*, Census Bureau (Washington, D.C.; 2000), table 57.

[12] This Census Bureau data was reported in *Pastor's Weekly Briefing* on May 12, 2000, page 2.

[13] These facts were drawn from several sources, including Census Bureau studies reported in *AFA Journal*, September 1998, page 9; research by Professor Susan Brown of Bowling Green State University, reported in *SAM Journal*, September-October 1998, page 28; and research by Professor Larry Bumpass of the University of Wisconsin, cited in *Newsweek*, November 2, 1998, page 60.

[14] Based on national studies conducted by the University of Michigan's Survey Research Center, reported in *Research Alert Yearbook 2000*, EPM Communications (New York: 2000), page 81.

[15] ibid

[16] The CDC and Guttmacher statistics were reported in *Pastor's Weekly Briefing*, January 16, 1998, page 2.

[17] Based on a national survey of adults by the Barna Research Group, conducted in May 2001 among 1003 adults.

[18] Based on data from a study by the Pew Research Center, a nationwide telephone survey conducted in October 2000.

[19] Based on a national survey of 1003 randomly selected adults, conducted by the Barna Research Group, May 2001.

[20] Based on a national survey of 1003 randomly selected adults, conducted by the Barna Research Group, May 2001.

[21] This information comes from the General Social Survey of 1998, conducted by NORC of the University of Chicago.

[22] This statistic was reported in the *AFA Journal*, September 1998, page 9.

[23] For more details on this study, consult the National Marriage Project research conducted by researchers at Rutgers University, in New Jersey. This survey entailed interviews with 1003 single adults in the 20 to 29-year old age group.

[24] Based on a national survey of 1003 randomly selected adults, conducted by the Barna Research Group, May 2001.

[25] Pew Research Center, a nationwide telephone survey conducted in March 2001.

[26] ibid

[27] Based on a national survey of adults by the Barna Research Group, conducted in May 2001 among 1003 adults.

[28] ibid

[29] ibid

Chapter 5
THE ROLL OF FAITH

Americans are known for their interest in religion. As the September 11 terrorist attack in 2001 brought to the fore, however, not everyone perceives America's faith to have influenced people's lives in a God-glorifying way.

Plenty of evidence exists to suggest that faith is an important influence in Americans' lives. Although the attention of single adults may be somewhat diverted to other interests, faith plays a significant role in their lives, too. Two out of three never-been-married people say they are "spiritual"; half of those who have never walked the aisle describe themselves as "deeply spiritual." The numbers are even higher for the rest of the singles mass. Three-quarters of both the widowed and divorced adults say they are spiritual. Three-fifths of the divorced and three-quarters of the widowed go so far as to portray themselves as "deeply spiritual." (Notice that among the widowed, it's generally an all-or-nothing deal: either you're deeply spiritual or you're not spiritual at all.)

But apart from thinking that they are spiritually inclined, how does faith work itself into their minds and hearts?

Feelings Towards Faith Groups

Most single adults are sufficiently aware of the major faiths to have developed some lasting impressions of each faith group. For the most part, Americans are both syncretic and tolerant when it comes to religion. In other words they have created their own unique system of beliefs that borrows bits and pieces of theological perspective from a variety of faith groups. Consequently, they are comfortable letting anyone believe pretty much whatever they want to believe. This creative theological approach and generous open-mindedness is fueled by the collapse of moral truth in the past century, and the concurrent rise of the notion that faith is an optional supplement to one's life rather than the foundation of it. In this way of thinking, every faith group is legitimate and everyone's truth is just as valid as everyone else's.

Consequently, virtually every faith group is seen as adding value to the mosaic of American society. Half or more of all single adults have positive feelings toward each of the major religious groups in the nation, with the exception of atheists (if you can consider them to be a faith group). Keep in mind, too, that most people have no idea what other faith groups believe or stand for, so their dominant impressions of almost every faith group beyond the one to which they belong are based on the few people they know who represent that group – or how the media have portrayed that group.

While anywhere between one-seventh to one-third of singles do not know enough about any given faith group to have an impression of it, when those who do have an opinion pass judgment, it is generally positive. Among those with an opinion on the group, 88% of singles have a favorable impression of Jews, 87% have a positive feeling about Catholics, and 81% have a positive outlook on evangelical Christians. Somewhat fewer singles – 71% – have a positive opinion toward Muslims in the U.S. (although that may have changed since the September 11 attack on America). The exception to the pattern of positive thinking relates to atheists. While Americans have become more comfortable with atheism over the years, a majority of people with an opinion on atheists (and that constitutes four out of five singles) lean toward the negative end of the continuum: only 44% have a favorable impression of atheists.

Singles' Opinions of Major Faith Groups[1]

| | no opinion | view of those with an opinion | |
		favorable	unfavorable
Evangelical Christians	23%	81%	19%
Jews	19	88	12
Catholics	14	87	13
Muslim Americans	30	71	29
Atheists	18	44	56

For the sake of context, the opinions of married people closely resemble those of unmarried adults. The primary difference is that married adults have even less favorable opinions of atheists.

Present-Day Alignments

Most single adults think of themselves as Christian, although their depth of commitment to the Christian faith varies considerably. Eight out of ten never-been-marrieds (78%) say they are Christian, which is slightly less than the 85% of divorced adults and 91% among widowed people. Very few singles claim to be atheists: 10% of those who have never wed, 6% of the divorced and only 4% of widowed citizens.[2]

The tepid alignment of the never-been-married niche with Christianity is complemented by a generally weak commitment to the Christian faith. When singles who claimed to be adherents of the Christian faith were asked to describe how committed they are to Christianity, only one out of every three never-married individuals (34%) said they were "absolutely committed." In comparison, half of divorced people who are self-described Christians (50%) said their commitment is absolute, and two-thirds of widowed Christians (68%) made the same affirmation.[3]

Why are never-been-married people so lukewarm toward Christianity? There is no simple or single reason for this. Among the chief reasons is the generational spiritual drift that is occurring these days, with young adults using spiritual language and symbols to develop a unique and positive persona, but without embracing the deeper content that such symbols have traditionally reflected. Another important reason is the acceptance of the post-modern philosophy that suggests there is no right or wrong, there is no particular faith that has a corner on truth or righteousness, and that all faiths are of equal value. This thinking has reduced the intensity of allegiance that young people have to a specific faith, be it Christianity, Islam or Buddhism. Add to this a generation-wide skepticism toward organizations and we have the makings of a population group who will lead America into the future without much sense of spiritual heritage or loyalty.

As the life stage of never-been-marrieds shifts from unmarried to married, a small proportion of the group will alter its thinking and move to a more traditional perspective on faith alignment and commitment. But with each passing generation we see a continued erosion of the depth of commitment to the Christian faith in America. We have no reason to believe that this pattern will suddenly change for the better.

Integrating the Pillars of the Faith

Single adults have developed an idiosyncratic view of what is important in one's faith emphasis. Examining the early church, as described in the Acts of the Apostles, it appears that the foundations of the church are six-fold: worship, evangelism, personal spiritual development, resource stewardship, community service and fellowship among believers. These are the pillars of the Christian faith, and constitute the dimensions of faith practice and development that form the basis of healthy Christians and churches. Yet, our research related to these pillars suggests that most churches and believers treat this list as a menu to choose from, rather than an integrated set of foci that cannot be broken into components. Americans, whether single or married, tend to identify one or two pillars with which they feel comfortable, and then focus upon developing themselves in those areas, resulting in incomplete and unbalanced believers. Churches fall prey to the same miscue, producing specialty or "boutique" churches that emphasize one or two pillars and pay lip service to the others.[4]

As we study reactions to the importance of each of eight emphases, we find that singles have generally developed a discernible sense of the relative significance of each of these faith dimensions.[5] Worship is easily perceived to be the most significant of these undertaking, as three-quarters of all single adults described worshiping God as very important. Learning about the content of one's faith trailed, with two-thirds labeling that activity as very important. Experiencing true spiritual and moral accountability and serving the needs of the poor were embraced by slightly more than half of all singles. About four out of ten unmarried people lumped evangelism, feeling as if you belong to a faith group, and meeting with others of the faith as highly significant tasks. Lowest on the list was material stewardship, cited by only one-third as very important.[6]

The Importance of Different Faith Emphases[7]
(% who said "very important")

faith emphasis	SLG	NBM	WID	DIV	MAR
worshiping God	74%	70%	85%	75%	78%
learning about the content of your faith	64	61	76	63	62
experiencing moral and spiritual accountability	57	52	73	58	61
serving the poor	56	50	73	54	55
sharing your faith with others	42	37	65	39	44
feeling like you belong to a faith group	38	33	48	38	44
meeting with other people of your faith	38	34	53	35	39
donating time and money to ministry	35	31	47	36	43

(Key: SGL = all single adults; NBM = never been married; WID = widowed; DIV = divorced; MAR = married)

However, there are substantial distinctions in the views that each singles niche has of each focus. In considering all eight of these emphases we can see that never-been-marrieds are the least excited about them (their average "very important" rating across the eight attributes was 46%), with divorced adults (average score of 50%) and their married counterparts (average score of 53%) slightly more convinced of the importance of these endeavors. Widowed adults were by far the most persuaded of the significance of these matters, with two-thirds of this group (65%, on average) citing each factor as "very important."

To assess the relative importance of each of these emphases in the eyes of the different singles segments, the table below provides an index for each of the factors. This analysis indicates that compared to all adults, not a single spiritual emphasis among the pillars for which never-been-married adults even reaches the national average. In other words, representatives of that singles niche are more complacent about all of these efforts than are other Americans. Learning the content of their faith is their "hot button," but even that is lukewarm. Emphases such as stewardship and feeling as if they belong to a faith group were the least compelling elements in their minds.

Widowed adults reside at the opposite end of the excitement continuum. Their levels of enthusiasm for each of the eight elements tested surpassed that of every other singles niche as well as that of married people. In relative terms, they seem most attracted to sharing their faith, serving others in need, and meeting with other people of their faith.

Divorced adults fall somewhere in-between the youngest and oldest singles niches on seven of the eight dimensions. That may give us insight into the reasons, too – the fact that age plays a significant part in determining the importance assigned by people to these endeavors. Since most divorced people are in their mid-thirties to mid-fifties, the "averageness" of their response may be as much a generational response as a personal, spiritual reflection.

An Index of the Importance of Different Faith Emphases[8]
(100 = national adult average)

faith emphasis	SLG	NBM	WID	DIV	MAR
worshiping God	99	93	113	100	104
learning about the content of your faith	102	97	121	100	98
having real moral and spiritual accountability	97	88	124	98	103
serving the poor	104	93	135	100	102
sharing your faith with others	95	84	148	89	100
feeling like you belong to a faith group	93	80	117	93	107
meeting with other people of your faith	97	87	136	90	100
donating time and money to ministry	90	79	121	92	110

(Key: SGL = all single adults; NBM = never been married; WID = widowed; DIV = divorced; MAR = married)

Overall, divorced adults are also relatively lukewarm on these areas of spiritual focus, failing to exceed the national average on any of the eight dimensions. The four aspects that seem least compelling to divorced people are evangelism, feeling like they belong, spending time with others in their faith group, and stewardship of resources.

Single adults, in essence, are searching for a church that will provide them with comfort, friends and some good information. There is shockingly little interest in pursuing real spiritual depth. One out of five single adults said what they want most from a church is to feel good or happy as a result of their engagement with the ministry; another one-fifth said they're seeking friends; and one out of every six want to know more about what the Bible says. (Divorced and widowed adults were nearly twice as likely as never-been-married singles to list Bible knowledge as a desirable product of their church participation.) Relatively few individuals are seeking any type of specific personal spiritual growth. An alarming one-quarter of the churched singles interviewed admitted that they had no idea what they want from their involvement with church.[9]

Intentional Spiritual Growth

Discussing the meaning of spiritual development with Americans is an interesting challenge. It became quite clear during our research that few adults – whether married or single, male or female, young or old, black, white or Hispanic, highly educated or illiterate, Protestant or Catholic – spend much time thinking about why or how they should grow spiritually. Most Americans are satisfied to go through the motions of their habitual spiritual practices, blindly assuming that repetition of those actions will please God and build up their self-esteem.

Most single adults state that they are on top of spiritual growth. Two-thirds of the never-been-married, and three-fourths of the divorced and widowed segments say they devote some of their personal time to growing or developing spiritually. There are, however, two distinct types of individuals who consider themselves to be Christian and engage in intentional spiritual development activity: those who pursue depth on a regular basis, and those who never or only rarely do so – there were very few individuals in-between the extremes. Among all self-described Christian singles, two out of five (41%) tend to engage in spiritual development practices in a typical week, one out of ten (11%) do so at least once a month but less often than weekly, and the other half does so infrequently, if at all.

Spiritual development is a two-sided coin: one side relates to intelligently pursuing growth and the other side relates to evaluating and redirecting that growth. Currently, only half of all self-professed Christian singles say their church has helped them to think through and identify specific, reasonable and measurable goals for spiritual growth. Even fewer single adults – just one-third of the never-married group and two-fifths of the remaining singles – say that they have any standards they use to help evaluate their personal spiritual vitality. In other words, most singles who consider themselves to be Christian and are at least tangentially involved in church life have almost no way of determining where they are going spiritually, whether or not they are making progress, and generally how mature they are spiritually.

A deeper examination of the standards relied upon by the minority who have such measurable factors in mind shows that their substance is not very helpful: the standards typically concern how many times they attend church or how many times they read the Bible. These are not bad things to measure, of course, but neither do they tell us much about the development of the person's mind, soul, or spirit. More than four out of five single adults lack any significant measures of their relationship with Christ, their commitment to practicing different, Spirit-led ways of life, or more consistently engaging with God in a deeply personal way.

In one national survey we asked people to describe what it means to grow spiritually. Their answers were quite revealing. Most single people gave us two or more ideas about the meaning of spiritual growth. However, the vast majority talked about general things that they might do; very few described what growth actually is or what types of life changes or personal outcomes they were seeking. Most often, we heard about events and activities, rather than the outcomes that they were pursuing, or specific evidence of positive spiritual development.

The most frequent responses dealt with common behaviors – reading the Bible, praying and attending church more regularly. A majority of single adults provided at least one of these activity-based answers. About three out of ten single adults listed some type of lifestyle change or evidence of spiritual depth, such as helping other people, demonstrating kindness or generosity, or being a better or more godly individual. Some people – roughly one out of every five – alluded to simply focusing on spirituality through discussion or seeking more information as an indication of spiritual growth. About one out of ten single adults admitted they had no idea what the concept means.

What "Spiritual Growth" Means to Singles[10]

meaning of personal spiritual growth	SGL	NBM	WID	DIV	MAR
to read or study the Bible	36%	38%	27%	41%	43%
to pray or have quiet times with God	33	39	25	31	35
to get more involved in church	16	18	10	19	17
to help others/volunteer	15	11	27	13	15
to show the fruit of the Spirit in my life	14	14	10	13	11
to interact with others about spirituality	13	10	14	16	14
to be a good or godly person	13	14	19	6	13
to gain more religious knowledge	12	9	15	14	15
don't know what it means	9	10	6	9	12

(Key: SGL = all single adults; NBM = never been married; WID = widowed; DIV = divorced; MAR = married)

One of the most disturbing revelations was the response to a question about the potential of church assistance in a more intensive discipling process. When asked how they would react to leaders in their church helping them to identify specific procedures and potential outcomes to pursue toward becoming a more mature Christian, one-third (36%) of all self-proclaimed Christians who attend church said they would welcome such advice and assistance; half said they would listen to some of the ideas offered, but would determine on their own what, if anything, to do with those suggestions; and the remainder said they would either ignore the advice or leave the church.

We have found consistently in related qualitative research that when spiritual leaders challenge people to get more serious about their faith in Christ, massive numbers of church people either turn a deaf ear or turn around and walk out the door, never to return. Helping believers to grow by introducing specific types of life change to shoot for and providing accountability for efforts to achieve such outcomes are not popular ideas.

The most damning evidence of all, however, has to do with the identity of what churched singles consider the most desirable outcomes of spiritual growth efforts. For most singles, the most desirable outcomes are self-focused, suggesting that a large number of self-described Christians who are single perceive spirituality to be anchored on self rather than God. Roughly half of all singles described the desired outcomes of spiritual investment to be emotional security (for example, "feeling good about myself," "feeling at peace with the world" or "feeling happy"); developing better relationships with other people (e.g., "feeling more connected to others," "having better friends," or "feeling like I'm part of a group of people who understand me"); and generic personal improvement (such as, "being a better person," or "improving my skills"). About half listed more plausible outcomes such as having a better relationship with God, knowing more content of the Bible, engaging in the spiritual disciplines, and having a meaningful personal ministry to other people. (One out of every four adults mixed the self-focused and God-focused outcomes into a very Americanized hybrid.) One-quarter of all self-described Christian singles said they have no idea what they want to achieve in terms of personal spiritual growth.

In essence, when singles who align themselves with the Christian faith think about where they are going with that faith, the group is divided into quadrants: one-quarter are completely selfish, thinking only about how they can use faith to further their worldly goals; one-quarter are focused solely on deepening their experience with God; one-quarter are juggling worldly and other-worldly objectives, striving to keep both ends in harmony; and one-quarter don't give spiritual growth a second thought, simply going through some religious routines until they achieve greater clarity about their life's meaning.

Gifted for Ministry

How sophisticated is the spiritual knowledge and commitment of singles? One measure suggests that the superficiality alluded to through the previously discussed measures is accurate. When we quizzed singles who describe themselves as Christian about spiritual gifts, we discovered that about seven out of ten had heard of spiritual gifts. Of those, just six out of ten never-been-marrieds and divorced adults, and eight out of ten widowed people claimed to possess a spiritual gift. Upon asking people to identify those gifts, the level of ignorance and misinformation was astounding.

A closer look at the data provides four important insights. First, even among the relatively few single adults who have heard of spiritual gifts, a large proportion do not know what theirs are. Second, the older a person is, the more likely they are to claim the presence of specific gifts, suggesting that many young people and young adults waltz through their first two or three decades of life ignorant of who they are and how God has prepared them to serve – potentially hindering not only their impact for His kingdom, but also their sense of value in God's eyes and uniqueness in His creation. Third, and most disheartening of all, is the fact that half of all single adults described "spiritual gifts" that are not the special abilities described in the Bible. Among the "spiritual gifts" claimed by singles were patience, good health, having children, musical ability, a nice apartment, dancing, tolerance and a fine radio!

The Spiritual Gifts Claimed by Single Adults[11]

(Base: single adults who consider themselves to be
Christian, say they have heard of spiritual gifts, and
believe God has given one or more gifts)

type of spiritual gifts mentioned	SGL	NBM	DIV	MAR
leadership-related gifts	6%	9%	5%	9%
communication-related gifts	13	9	20	17
revelation-related gifts	19	14	23	13
outreach-related gifts	8	6	14	18
service-related gifts	10	8	11	20
non-biblical gifts	47	49	52	48
have gifts but don't know what they are	19	18	14	10

Definitions:
leadership-related: apostle, administration, leadership, shepherd, pastor communication-related: encouragement, exhortation, teaching
revelation-related: discernment, interpretation, knowledge, prophecy, tongues, wisdom
outreach-related: evangelism, healing, hospitality, intercession, mercy
service-related: giving, helps
(Key: SGL = all single adults; NBM = never been married; DIV = divorced;
MAR = married)

In total, 12% of all singles listed only biblical spiritual gifts, 14% solely listed non-biblical gifts, 2% listed a combination of biblical and non-biblical gifts, and six out of ten single adults have no idea about gifts (either because they do not label themselves Christian, they have never heard of gifts or they believe God has not given them a gift).[12]

Imagine what might happen if single adults were better informed about how God has entrusted a special gift or combination of gifts to each of His followers. The informed application of those gifts in life and ministry could radically change the self-perception, the spiritual fervor and the kingdom impact of tens of millions of unmarried people. We ought not wait until these people are in their twenties, thirties or forties to broach the topic. Teaching young believers about their gifts, and helping them to find ways to hone and use those special abilities as they age, would have an incredible impact upon their lives and the world in which they serve.

But the present condition – i.e., most single adults are clueless about gifts – is indicative of a much deeper and more serious problem: the spiritual complacency and ignorance of single adults. Knowing about spiritual gifts is of little value to a person who does not see himself or herself as created to love God through personal purity, worship and devotion to God, and service to others.

Fatuous Faith

Consider this: less than five out of every 100 single adults in America is absolutely committed to the Christian faith, is actively seeking to grow in each of the pillar areas of spirituality, regularly invests himself or herself in intentional spiritual growth efforts, and can identify and give evidence of using their spiritual gifts to serve God and His people. The percentage of never-been-married singles that fit this description represents only half the number found from among widowed and divorced adults, but in every singles niche we studied, the proportion is in the single digits. Clearly, there is much growth yet to be accomplished!

Footnotes

[1] These figures are from a national telephone survey conducted September 2000 by the Pew Research Center.

[2] This is based on interviews across the nation with 2847 single adults from January 2000 through July 2001, via telephone, by the Barna Research Group.

[3] ibid

[4] A more extensive discussion of the integration of these pillars into vital ministry is contained in my book *The Habits of Highly Effective Churches* (Regal Books: Ventura, CA; 1999). We discovered that the churches where people's

lives are being transformed to greater Christ-likeness have nine key habits – a focus on the six pillars plus three habits that facilitate the development of mature faith in those areas.

[5] The discussion here centers on the six pillars of the faith, but analyses reactions to eight aspects of faith pursuit. The reason for the discrepancy in the number of elements discussed is that both the discipleship and fellowship functions were broken into two elements to more completely convey their substance.

[6] Based on a national telephone survey by the Barna Research Group in November 2000 with a random sample of 1002 adults, including 479 singles.

[7] ibid

[8] ibid

[9] Based on a national telephone survey by the Barna Research Group in January 2000 with a random sample of 1004 adults, including 469 singles.

[10] Based on a national telephone survey by the Barna Research Group in May 2000 with a random sample of 1003 adults, including 458 singles.

[11] ibid

[12] ibid

Chapter 6
THE RELIGIOUS PRACTICES OF SINGLES

A few years ago, a phrase from the movie Jerry Maguire, spoken by a pro football player to his ever-promising, never-delivering agent, captured the imagination of the American people and became part of the daily lexicon: "Show me the money!" The public related to the player's fatigue with unfulfilled albeit good intentions; he simply wanted his agent to make good on his promises.

In the same way, we might imagine God observing all the posturing about religiosity and listening to the omnipresent talk about spirituality in America, pursing His lips, shaking His head and bellowing from on-high, "Show me the faith!"

Jesus harshly criticized those who played the religious game but failed to live the spiritual life. For Him, the proof is in the practice: talking the game is not nearly as crucial as walking the talk. How deeply have single adults invested themselves in actions that might bear spiritual fruit?

For younger singles, involvement is a more unique commitment, since fewer of them grew up in families that regularly involved them in spiritual endeavors. Less than six out of ten (57%) never-been-married adults regularly attended a Christian church when they were growing up, compared to three out of four among divorced adults and eight out of ten widowed individuals.[1] Given our recent research that shows the dramatic affect on adult religiosity of attending church when young, the lack of religious routines and experiences among the never-been-marrieds puts them at a distinct spiritual disadvantage.

Relationship With A Church

In a typical week, slightly more than one out of every three single adults attend a church service. Presence at a church service is much more likely among widowed adults (half are present on an average weekend) than among divorced people (slightly more than one-third of whom attend) or never-been-married adults (not quite three out of ten). The oft-heard complaint of single adults – "church is for married couples and families" – may well be attributed to the fact that married people and their children are more likely to show up at church than are singles: 51% of married adults attend a church service in a typical week, which is nearly 50% higher than the probability of singles appearing in the pews. Add to that the reality that married adults bring more people with them, and that they donate greater sums of money and hours of volunteer labor, and the alleged bias toward families is more understandable, although not justifiable.[2]

Single adults cannot make the argument that their unique lifestyle simply makes them too busy or too committed to other responsibilities to enable them to attend church. In a survey conducted between six and eight weeks after the terrorist attacks in 2001, church attendance had declined somewhat from the unnaturally high levels the first two weeks after the attacks, but was still slightly above the norm: four out of ten never-been-marrieds, six out of ten widowed folks, and slightly more than four out of ten divorced adults. (The proportion of married adults attending was little changed, clocking in at 55% - only a few percentage points higher than their pre-attack average.)[3]

The churches that single adults have chosen to associate with are somewhat different than those that attract married adults. About one-fifth of singles and married folks attend Baptist churches. One-quarter of married people associate with mainline Protestant congregations, compared to just one-eighth of never-been-marrieds, one-fifth of the divorced, and nearly one-third of the widowed. (Put differently, widowed singles are more than twice as likely to align with mainline churches as are the younger, never-married singles.) Never-been-marrieds are the most likely singles niche to attend a Catholic church (28%, compared to 19% of widowed and 22% of divorced people, and 26% of married adults). Comparatively few single adults – one out of twenty – attend non-denominational churches, although the proportion that does so is identical to that of married adults.[4]

Surprisingly, single adults are more likely than married adults to attend a small church. Most unexpected of all is that divorced adults are the most likely singles segment to attend a church with less than 100 adults in average attendance. Only one out of ten single adults go to a megachurch, compared to one out of eight among married people. A key reason for the attraction of larger churches among married people is the presence of a larger and assumedly better-quality children's ministry. Given the paucity of significant singles ministry offerings at most smaller churches, one might imagine that single adults are not as likely to view a church as a place to meet a potential mate as was the case a couple of decades ago.[5]

Weekly Religious Activity

It is important to make a distinction between the quantity of religious activities undertaken and the quality or impact of those experiences. If we focus on the amount of religious activity that occurs in the lives of single adults, the sheer volume of time and energy devoted to religious involvement is enormous – not as widespread as would be desired, of course, but substantial nevertheless.

The only activity of the eight measured for which a majority are involved in a typical week is praying to God, an act that four out of five single adults claim to engage in. Half of all singles have a quiet time or private devotional time during the average week. Only one-third of the unmarried population attends church services during a typical week, and the same proportion reads from the Bible other than at church. Less than one out of five single adults volunteers at church, attends a Sunday school class, or participates in a small group or cell group during an average week. Significantly, singles are 50% more likely to volunteer their services to a non-profit or charitable group other than a church during a typical week than they are to offer themselves to the ministry of their church.

Each singles segment experienced different levels of activity and relative involvement. The never-been-married group was the least likely of the three major singles subgroups to be engaged in spiritual activities;

in fact, this segment was the least likely to participate in six of the eight efforts measured, and was tied for lowest involvement on the other two. There was only one activity that at least half of the never-married folks engaged in – prayer – and just one other endeavor that attracted more than one-third of them in a typical week — having a personal quiet time. Even though devotional times were the second-rated activity among this group, they were the only marital-segment studied among whom less than half were so inclined. Never-been-marrieds were nearly twice as likely to volunteer at a non-profit or charity than at a church. And despite their relatively young age, and their interest in finding a "soul mate," just one out of seven from this niche involved themselves in a small group. Given their alleged interest in spirituality and relationships, this proportion – again, lowest among the four marital segments examined – is surprising, but underscores the overemphasis analysts have placed on the spiritual commitment of young adults.

The Religious Practices of Americans in a Typical Week[6]

religious activity in past 7 days	SGL	NBM	WID	DIV	MAR
read from the Bible, other than at church	36%	29%	52%	39%	42%
attended a church service, other than special event	35	29	49	37	51
volunteered to help at a church	18	14	28	20	29
volunteered free time to help a non-profit organization, other than a church or synagogue	27	24	28	30	32
prayed to God	80	74	90	85	84
attended a Sunday school class	15	13	24	14	23
participated in a small group, other than a Sunday school class or 12-step group, that meets regularly, for Bible study, prayer or Christian fellowship	15	14	22	15	21
spent some quiet time by yourself, reading the Bible or devotional literature and praying, other than while you were at church	50	40	72	57	54

(Key: SGL = all single adults; NBM = never been married; WID = widowed; DIV = divorced; MAR = married)

101

Widowed adults showed the most active involvement in a range of religious pursuits. In fact, they ranked highest among the three singles niches on all eight of the endeavors tracked. They were more likely than married adults to engage in three of the eight activities, and were equally likely in relation to the other five. More than half of all widowed people read the Bible, attend church, pray and have a private devotional time during an average week. They are twice as likely as other singles to attend a Sunday school class; almost two-thirds more likely to have a personal devotional time; and about 60% more likely to read the Bible than are other singles.

Divorced adults held the middle ground on five of the eight items when compared to never-been-married and widowed singles. The only two actions that more than half of divorced adults engage in during a typical week are praying to God and having a personal devotional time. Overall, divorced people are somewhat skeptical about church life because of how the congregation will respond to their marital status.

Compared to married adults, singles are less likely to be involved in each of the eight activities assessed. The biggest gaps related to endeavors such as church attendance (a 16-point differential); church volunteerism (11-point gap); and Sunday school attendance (an 8-point distinction).

Many social analysts suggested that the terrorist attack on America had changed the spiritual tenor and fervor of the nation. Our research showed that not to be the case. Based on a national study conducted two months after the terrorist attack we found that the religious practices of Americans, including singles, had barely changed. Immediately after the attack a huge surge occurred in church attendance, and that remained the last vestige of the attack, recorded at nine percentage points above the pre-attack level for singles, escalating to 44% those who attend during a typical week. Prayer, Sunday school attendance, voluntarism, small group involvement and devotional times all remained static. The number of single adults who volunteered their time to a church continued to trail the proportion of singles who volunteered their time to other non-profits and charitable organizations (29%). Within each of the segments, never-been-marrieds were the only group to increase its church volunteer efforts (jumping from 14% to 21% – a small aggregate, but a 50% increase from the pre-attack level) and involvement in a small group also rose by six percentage points. Widowed people exhibited a substantial decrease in quiet times, dropping from 72% to 61%. Divorced people showed the greatest rise in Bible reading (up six points) and Sunday school attendance (up 11 points). For the most part, however, the levels of activity remained surprisingly consistent after the attack.[7]

Less Frequent Religious Activity

Among the activities we measure on a monthly basis are financial support (since people's paychecks arrive at different intervals and thus affect giving patterns). We found that within a typical month, a bit less than half of all singles donate some money to a church. The usual pattern is evident across the three primary singles segments: widowed adults are most likely to donate (66%), followed by divorced people (50%) and lagged by the never-been-marrieds (34%). For context, realize that two-thirds of married adults (64%) donate money to a church during an average month.[8]

We also learned that singles are nearly as likely to give money to other non-profits, besides churches, as they are to support a community of faith. Nearly four out of ten singles (37%) gave to other non-profits and charities in a typical month. Again, widowed people lead the way (52% give to such causes), followed by divorced people (45%), and distantly tailed by the never-been-marrieds (29%). Half of all married adults give to non-church organizations during a typical month.

Consider the following four insights related to giving. First, most never-been-marrieds do not give anywhere. Second, both divorced and never-married people are nearly as likely to give to non-church entities as to support a church. Third, despite their limited incomes and even more limited likelihood of seeing their income rise, widowed people are the most generous singles. Finally, comparing these figures to similar data from a decade earlier, the pattern emerges of increased resistance to church giving: in 1991, never-been-married and divorced singles were more likely to donate to a church than they are to do so today. For the most part we are examining the behavior of completely different people who are in similar marital states, yet how people in those segments relate to churches and their money has changed significantly.

The amounts of money donated to churches and non-profits over the course of a year vary considerably, too. The mean amount given to churches in calendar year 2000 ranged from just $239 among the never-been-married segment, to $412 among the divorced, $570 among the widowed, and $1023 among married people. In related fashion, we found that two-thirds of never-been-marrieds donated something to a church, three-quarters of the widowed followed suit, and four out of five divorced adults displayed some generosity. All three segments, however, were shown-up by married adults: 85% donated funds to a church in 2000. Among those who give anything to a church, most of their giving winds up in church coffers: about 59% of the funds given by church-supporting never-been-marrieds, 71% of the giving of widowed people, and 80% of the funds contributed by divorced adults. Married people barely led the pack, giving 81% of their total donations to churches.

We also track people's engagement in evangelism. Generally speaking, single adults are just as likely as married people to share their faith in Christ with a non-believer during the year. Slightly less than six out of ten born again adults, whether single or married, had done so during each of the past several years. Breaking the established pattern, the group most likely to have shared their faith was the never-been-married contingent. (Keep in mind, however, that this is based upon a subset of each singles population – those who are born again Christians.)[9]

Finally, we explored the act of holding a leadership position in a church. Married adults were about 50% more likely to hold such posts than were single adults. Among the singles, just one out of eight were involved in such an act of service, most often in a teaching capacity. The differences among the singles niches were huge, though: only 7% of the never-been-married group held a leadership position, compared to 11% of the divorced and 29% of the widowed. These figures do not reflect people's *willingness* to serve in a leadership position, but whether or not they were invited to do so by their church and then agreed to fill the position.

Understanding the Unchurched

About three out of ten single adults are unchurched, defined as not having attended a Christian church service, other than a holiday service or a special event such as a wedding or funeral, within the past six months.

The subgroups within the singles population who are most likely to abstain from church attendance are men, singles who do not have a college degree, residents of the Northeast and West, and Protestants.

Half of the unchurched singles in our nation are unable to recall the name of even one church located within 15 minutes of their home. Combined with the revelation that most unchurched singles have never been invited by a churched person to attend a church service, we can posit church life is not on the minds of most unchurched singles.

The research also shows that we often misunderstand how unchurched people want to be treated should they choose, for whatever reason, to visit a church. Most unchurched people want to be left alone when they visit, except for receiving a genuine greeting from church regulars either before or after the service, a thank you note from the pastor within the week following their attendance, and the opportunity to pick up some background information about the church without any sales pitch or other pressure accompanying that information. They do not want to be singled-out for special attention, they don't want special gifts and they don't want to defend their presence at the church by explaining why they're visiting or who brought them. They want to come, check out the people, and develop a visceral response to an emotional experience, rather than develop a mental response to an intellectual experience.

The Future Church: Going Online

As technology becomes an increasingly ingrained aspect of American life, you can expect a growing number of people to turn to the Internet for spiritual experiences and expression. By the end of this decade, close to one out of every ten Americans will have completely rejected the bricks-and-mortar church in favor of a cyberchurch experience. While this movement will be generational more than familial in character, we can already see that this mindset is affecting ministry particularly among those who today are in the never-been-married category – many of whom will be in the divorced category a decade from now.

Currently, most single adults contend that they are more likely to have a superior spiritual experience, regardless of what spiritual dynamic is studied (e.g., worship, discipleship, service, stewardship) through the physical church than through the cyberchurch. The aspects of spirituality for which the Internet is likely to be deemed a better vehicle than the physical church include evangelism and Christian education; but even for these areas barely one out of eight singles would argue that the Internet is more conducive than a physical church to a positive experience. That is one reason why few singles say they are likely to completely abandon the physical church in place of the cyberchurch.

But people have a terrible track record of predicting personal change. We believe that the acceptance of the cyberchurch will be just one more example of people not realizing that they will shift their allegiance over the course of time. Most people will not make that shift during our lifetime, but a substantial number of single (and married) adults are already engaged in a process of making this shift.

A key example of this unforeseen change of emphasis is evident by exploring how likely single adults say they are, even during this early era in the nascent history of the cyberchurch, to use the Internet to satisfy each of a number of spiritual needs. As you examine the figures in the accompanying table, you will see a substantial existing openness toward, and expectation of using the Internet to help them fulfill their spiritual quest.

Half of all adults, single and married, expect to use the Internet to access religious teaching archived on a website, listened to via audio-streaming technology whenever the mood strikes. Not surprisingly, never-been-married adults, who are more technology-savvy than their older single counterparts, are the segment most likely to engage in such activity.

About nine out of every twenty single adults currently plan to use the Internet to submit prayer requests, and to access short religious readings that will motivate, focus or challenge the individual.

Four out of ten singles, led by the never-been-married group, expect to use the Net to purchase books and study guides regarding religion and matters of faith.

One out of three single people (37%) plan to use the Internet to engage in an online, independent study course that focuses on faith matters. A similar proportion expect to use the Net as the medium through which they will be Christian or religious music in the near future.

Three out of ten unmarried adults say they will use the Internet to participate in a chat room or discussion group online that focuses on religious matters; to engage in a real-time online Bible study group; to participate in an online class that meets regularly to study some particular aspect of religion or faith; and to gain coaching in spirituality by a more mature believer. In each of these dimensions the never-been-married group is most enthusiastic, while the older singles display muted anticipation.

The least enthralling spiritual possibility to singles is the prospect of real-time worship experienced online via a video-streaming process. Only 17% of all singles expressed interest in this potential ministry avenue.

Ways In Which Adults Expect to Use the Internet
to Meet Their Spiritual Needs[10]

way in which they could use the Internet	SGL	NBM	WID	DIV	MAR
to listen to religious teaching contained in an archives of teachings that you could access whenever you want, on whatever topic is of interest to you	51%	54%	41%	46%	50%
submit prayer requests to a group that prays for people's needs	45	48	36	41	35
read a short religious reading to motivate, challenge or focus you	44	49	31	42	45
buy books or study guides about religion or faith	41	45	27	41	42
participate in an online, independent study course related to faith matters	37	41	28	33	32
buy religious music	34	38	24	28	30
participate in a chat room or online discussion group regarding religion or faith	31	36	21	25	21
participate in a Bible study that takes place online, in real time	30	33	25	25	27
participate in an online class that meets regularly, online, to study some aspect of faith or religion	30	33	23	27	29
be mentored or coached in spiritual development by a person whose faith is more developed than yours	29	29	21	28	22
worship God through a real-time, video streaming worship experience	17	17	11	18	13

(Key: SGL = all single adults; NBM = never been married; WID = widowed; DIV = divorced; MAR = married)

When all of these levels of probable future involvement in religious activity are put together, we find that more than four out of five single adults have some aspect of faith or spirituality in mind for which they expect the Internet to be their source of substance or experience. As the years pass and the Internet becomes established as a standard component in our daily experience, and as technology itself evolves to facilitate a higher quality religious experience online, these figures will rise steadily. The cyberchurch will grow slowly but consistently as people become accustomed to online experiences related to faith, as other dimensions of our life make digital experiences a more common and socially acceptable substitute for more traditional experiences, and as the technology improves.

Investing in the Spirit

There are two levels on which we might assess the spiritual involvement of single adults. On the absolute level, in which we consider people's personal spiritual investment in comparison to biblical standards, we would have to conclude that relatively few Americans, married or not, are intensely committed to being true disciples of Christ. On a less stringent level, in which we compare singles to married adults, we must note that the higher levels of spiritual investment by married folks certify that a deeper level of involvement is feasible. Clearly, single adults lack a compelling motivation to abandon the world and devote themselves to the things of God. Finding those hot buttons that will encourage single adults to reorient their priorities and invest in their spirituality is, as the apostle Paul would say, "a worthy goal."

Footnotes

[1] Based on a nationwide telephone survey by the Barna Research Group in January 2001, with a random sample of 1003 adults, including 504 single adults.

[2] These figures come from an analysis of eight national quarterly tracking studies of church attendance by the Barna Research Group, involving more than 8000 adults and 3817 single adults, from January 2000 through November 2001.

[3] This national survey by Barna Research was conducted in October-November 2001 among 1001 adults, of whom 496 were singles.

[4] These statistics are drawn from a compilation of studies between January 2000 and July 2001 which involved 3148 married adults and 2847 single adults. All of these national telephone surveys were based upon random samples.

[5] ibid

[6] ibid

[7] Based on a nationwide telephone survey by the Barna Research Group in October-November 2001, with a random sample of 1001 adults, including 496 single adults.

[8] All of the giving data for 2000 are from the Barna Research annual tracking study of giving patterns conducted each January. This particular survey, exploring the behaviors of a national random sample of 1002 adults, included 504 singles.

[9] These statistics are drawn from a compilation of studies between January 2000 and July 2001 which involved 3148 married adults and 2847 single adults. All of these national telephone surveys were based

[10] This national survey by Barna Research was conducted in November 2000 among 1003 adults, a random sample that included 479 singles. For a more extensive exploration of the role of the Internet on people's faith, consult a research report entitled *The Cyberchurch*, prepared by The Barna Institute in 2001.

Chapter 7
WHAT SINGLE ADULTS BELIEVE

What we believe about God, truth, and faith matters – a lot. Understanding people's beliefs is critical to influencing them, because these are the bases on which they develop their core values. Those values, in turn, direct personal behavior.

Despite claims that we live in a "Christian nation," or that more than four out of five Americans consider themselves to be Christian, or evidence that more than 85% of the places of worship in America are dedicated to the pursuit of the Christian faith, we cannot afford to fall for such superficial diagnoses of the nation's spiritual condition. America is no more a Christian nation than China is a democracy. True, we have elements of Christian heritage and there are millions of dedicated Christians in the country and we are relatively comfortable with Christian symbols and language. But in the place where it really counts – our hearts – we are far removed from the type of Christian faith, experience and lifestyle that Jesus spoke of during His brief ministry on earth.

Turning to the Bible

Like other citizens, most single adults – nine out of ten of them – own a Bible. However, the first red flag we encounter relates to the version of the Bible most of them rely upon for insight into God's Word: the King James Version (KJV). Although married adults are slightly more likely than are singles to use the KJV as their primary version, about one-third of singles use this 400-year old translation. Four times as many single adults use the KJV as use the next most popular version (which is the New International Version, or NIV). There is nothing inappropriate about owning and using a KJV, of course – except for the fact that most Americans do not possess the literacy skills to adequately interpret the language used in the KJV. One must wonder what would happen if more single adults were introduced to more contemporary, reader-friendly translations of the Bible.

We can reasonably expect that a more accessible version would increase singles' reading of the Bible, and maybe even their enjoyment, appreciation and comprehension of its content. Currently, just one out of eight single adults reads the Bible on a daily basis; one in five reads it less than daily but at least weekly; two out of four read it one to three times each month; only a handful read the Bible infrequently, but three out of ten never read it.

Perhaps a different version of the scriptures would influence what single adults believe about the Bible itself. Presently, one-quarter contends that the Bible is the actual word of God, to be taken literally, word for word. A similar proportion argues that the Bible is the inspired word of God, containing no errors, but including some symbolism. One out of six say that the Bible is the inspired word of God that contains some historical and factual errors. Lesser numbers believe that it is not an inspired book but a collection of views held by the authors of each book (one out of ten), or that it is a book of teachings from men in the form of stories or advice (one-eighth). (Surprisingly, this profile differs little from that of married adults.)

Indisputably the best argument for transitioning millions of single adults to a more reader-friendly version of the Bible is because of what they think the Bible teaches. Most singles have a head full of theological notions. One must wonder, though, about the source of such musings, for it certainly is not the Bible.

Beliefs About the Bible

In addition to whether they think the Bible is inerrant or inspired, the research shows that a slim majority of single adults (53%) believes that the Bible is "accurate in all that it teaches." However, it is also important to note that a minority of singles - just one-third – strongly affirms the accuracy of the Bible's teachings, ranging from 31% of never-been-marrieds to 41% of the divorced and 46% of the widowed.[1] People groups within the singles universe most likely to believe in the accuracy of Bible content are women (41% strongly affirm the Bible's accuracy, compared to just 30% of single men); blacks (57% firmly argue that Scriptural teaching is accurate, nearly double the 32% of white singles who feel similarly); and people who do not have a college degree (40% strongly agree with this idea compared to just 30% of the singles who have a college degree). Protestant singles are twice as likely as Catholic singles to strongly affirm the complete accuracy of the Bible's teachings (51% versus 25%, respectively).

One of the most common distortions of biblical teaching is the notion that the Bible literally contains the principle that "God helps those who help themselves." The three-fourths of married folk who agree with this idea are not alone in their erroneous thinking: the same proportion of single adults buys into this view. In fact, a majority of single adults (55%) strongly agrees that this is a notion found in the Bible. For unknown reasons, this idea is more widely accepted by divorced adults (67% strongly believe the perspective is stated in Scripture) than by widowed (52%) or never-been-married people (48%).

Beliefs About Sin, Forgiveness, Salvation and Evangelism

Singles embrace a mixed bag of beliefs related to sin and salvation. To their credit, most believe that sin is still a relevant concept for our day. Only one out of every 14 single adults strongly argues that sin is an outdated concept; at the other end of the continuum, six out of ten strongly affirm that sin remains relevant to this day. Although young singles are the least likely to accept the concept of sin, a majority firmly defends its significance for understanding modern life.

Few single adults are aware of, or understand the contradiction between saying that there is no absolute moral truth on which to base daily choices and yet sin exists. Is sin therefore a relative reality: that is, what is sin for me may not be sin for you? Our research on this matter clearly demonstrates that few people have thought about the relationship of sin, goodness, truth and salvation. In fact, as postmodernism becomes a more entrenched philosophy in America, people are becoming more comfortable with such contradictions and feel less of a need to reconcile views that cannot co-exist.

Despite accepting the reality of sin, many single adults also embrace the mistaken notion that all people will experience the same outcome after they die, regardless of whether they had accepted Jesus Christ as their savior or not. Four out of ten singles believe this notion, less by half of the never-been-marrieds. (Only one-third of the widowed and two-fifths of the divorced concur.) A slightly higher proportion of single adults – half – disagrees that everyone will have the same eternal outcome.

The appeal of such universalistic thinking relates to the widespread notion that all faiths teach the same lessons, thereby eliminating the distinctiveness of any particular faith, and making acceptance of a faith group more significant than the identity and unique attributes of the group with which you associate. A slightly higher proportion of single adults (half) accepts the idea that all of the world's major religions teach the same basic lessons, while about four out of ten unmarried Americans reject that notion. Young singles are least likely to reject this notion: just one out of four singles under 35 strongly disagrees that all faiths teach the same core truths.

These ideas result in tainted beliefs about the possibility of, and means to eternal salvation. Fifty-five percent of all single adults agree that "if a person is basically good, or does enough good things for other people he or she will earn their way into Heaven." Only one out of four single adults firmly disagrees with good deeds as the route to salvation. This belief also illuminates a critical misunderstanding among most Americans, namely that people are inherently good. Scripture informs us that once sin invaded our hearts, we ceased to be pure – and sin is endemic to all human beings. Jesus did not have to die a cruel, unjust, humiliating and painful death on a cross because we are good people, but because we are wicked, perverse, sinful beings at heart. Only through spiritual rebirth that comes from accepting Christ as our savior and inviting the Holy Spirit to control our lives does the potential for goodness take on any significant meaning in our lives.

Four out of five single adults believe that God has given people free will and that, in turn, enables people to choose their eternal destiny. Six out of ten singles feel quite strongly about this freedom to choose; it fits snuggly into the American mold of self-determinism and a desire to have control and multiple options from which to make such choices.

Regarding salvation, most Americans, married or not, claim to have made a personal commitment to Jesus Christ that is still important in their lives these days. Six out of ten single adults make such a claim, as do half of all never-been-marrieds, and seven out of ten widowed and divorced adults. This is a curious claim in light of other admissions by these same people, such as the fact that many do not describe themselves as absolutely committed to the Christian faith or that they do not view their religious faith as very important in their lives today.

When those who claim such a personal commitment to Christ are asked about life after death, we find that making a personal commitment to Jesus and trusting Him for salvation are two different matters. Among the six out of ten who say they are committed to Christ, only a little more than half of them (57%) say that they are certain they will go to Heaven after they die solely because they have confessed their sins and have accepted Jesus to be their savior.

In essence, that means only one-third of single adults (35%) have become "born again" – that is, they no longer trust in their own good deeds as a means to reconciliation with God, but rely completely upon God's grace through Christ's death and resurrection on their behalf. Never-been-married adults are the least likely to meet the "born again" criteria: only 29% qualify. Higher proportions of widowed (44%) and divorced

(42%) adults are born again, but fewer people from all three niches qualify than is true among married adults (47%).[2]

We have also discovered that Hispanic singles are less likely to be born again (22% fit this classification) than are white (35%) or black (48%) singles. The two factors most responsible for this are the traditional Catholic background of most Hispanics (placing a substantial focus on personal effort as a means to earning God's favor, along with prayer to Mary and other saints) and their youthfulness (most Hispanics in America are under 40 years of age). Nationally, only 19% of Catholic singles are born again, compared to 54% of Protestant singles. The age factor is also undeniable. Only 28% of the singles under 35 are born again, compared to 38% of those who are 35 to 49 years of age, 42% of those in the 50 to 64 age bracket, and 44% of the 65 and older crowd.

Americans who claim commitment to Christ have all kinds of ideas regarding their eternal destiny. Among single adults who have made such a commitment, 17% admit that they do not know what will happen to them after they die. Ten percent say that they will be in Heaven because they were basically a good person on earth. Lesser percentages of singles who claim to be committed to Christ say they will be in Heaven because God loves all of the people He created and will not allow any of them to perish (7%), or because they have done a stellar job of obeying the Ten Commandments (5%). About 3% have other, idiosyncratic views.

Here's the kicker: just 1% believe that they will go to Hell. Americans will talk about sin, forgiveness, grace, salvation, and the like, but most Americans cannot bring themselves to face the possibility that they might live their post-flesh lives in a state of adversity with the God of all creation.

As for the connection between salvation and evangelism, there is some good news and some bad news in this story. The bad news is that most single adults are not relying upon Christ for their salvation. The good news is that most singles do not feel they have a responsibility to share their religious beliefs with individuals who see things differently than they do. Only three out of ten singles strongly believe that they have a duty to share their faith with others – and most of those people are born again Christians. The waters will be muddier than we might like, however, since four out of ten singles who embrace the responsibility to share their spiritual beliefs are not born again. If you hope to motivate believers to share Christ with others, the singles most likely to get excited about the challenge are women, blacks, and people 50 or older. Single adults under the age of 35 are especially reluctant to proselytize their friends; tolerance, diversity and postmodernism have made efforts to influence people's thinking about faith a cultural no-no.

The Trinity and the Adversary

Two out of three single adults have an orthodox, biblical view of God. Given a set of six possible views of God, the most popular choice is the description of God as an "all-powerful, all-knowing, perfect Creator of the universe who rules the world today." Six out of ten never-been-married adults adopt that view, compared to seven out of ten other single and married adults. Other views of God are less prolific. Eleven percent claim "god represents a state of higher consciousness that a person may reach." One out of 12 singles (8%) suggest, "God refers to the total realization of all human potential." Four percent say that everyone is God; 3% believe that "there are many gods, each with different power and authority"; and 3% say there is no such thing as God. Five percent don't know what to think.

What Americans Believe[3]

perspective	SGL	NBM	WID	DIV	MAR
the Bible is totally accurate in all of its teachings					
agree strongly	37%	31%	46%	41%	45%
agree somewhat	16	18	14	15	16
disagree somewhat	22	24	19	21	19
disagree strongly	19	22	11	17	15
don't know	6	6	9	5	6
personally have a responsibility to tell other people your religious beliefs					
agree strongly	28	24	36	31	36
agree somewhat	16	17	16	16	17
disagree somewhat	23	25	22	21	19
disagree strongly	30	33	22	31	27
don't know	2	2	5	2	2
your religious faith is very important in your life					
agree strongly	64	56	79	70	72
agree somewhat	19	22	13	17	15
disagree somewhat	9	12	5	7	7
disagree strongly	7	8	3	5	5
don't know	1	2	1	1	1
the devil, or Satan, is not a living being but is simply a symbol of evil					
agree strongly	41	39	44	43	37
agree somewhat	20	23	15	16	18
disagree somewhat	9	10	8	8	8
disagree strongly	23	23	23	23	31
don't know	7	6	10	9	7
if a person is generally good, or does enough good things for others during their life, they will earn a place in Heaven					
agree strongly	34	34	35	31	31
agree somewhat	21	24	17	18	17
disagree somewhat	12	12	11	14	11
disagree strongly	25	23	27	28	34
don't know	8	7	10	9	7
when He lived on earth, Jesus Christ was human and committed sins, like other people					
agree strongly	25	27	20	25	22
agree somewhat	21	24	16	18	18
disagree somewhat	9	10	7	9	8
disagree strongly	36	31	46	40	45
don't know	9	8	12	8	8
Number of respondents	2847	1576	446	700	3148

(Key: SGL = all single adults; NBM = never been married; WID = widowed; DIV = divorced; MAR = married)

These statistics indicate that nearly three out of ten single adults embrace a "new age" perspective on the nature of God. Most of those who reject a biblical perspective of God perceive deity to be a state of personal development rather than the existence of a holy being with dominion over humanity. Single males are more likely than single females to embrace such a view (27% vs. 22%, respectively); and singles under 35 years of age are more likely than their older unmarried peers to buy into such a concept (27% do so). Black singles were the least likely to embrace the new age view (14%). Amazingly, one out of every twelve born again singles has a new age portrait of "god" in mind.

Oddly, seven out of ten single adults strongly agree that God created the universe, and 85% agree either strongly or somewhat in the creation view. (This is "odd" because less than that proportion believe in God as an omnipotent Creator. Perhaps a slice of the unmarried population accept the view that God created the world but is no longer involved in it – a notion popular in some theological circles, and which would have appeal to some singles, given their overall spiritual perspective.)

One out of three singles are willing to limit God's power by suggesting that there are some sins that not even God Himself can forgive. In fact, only half of the singles universe believes strongly that this view is incorrect – further evidence that Americans are relatively confused about God, His purposes, His power and His plans.

Even fuzzier thinking prevails when it comes to the reality of Jesus Christ. While most singles contend that Jesus was a real, historical figure, half also contends that He committed sins while He was on earth. This view is much more common among young singles and those who have never-been-married than among older singles and those who have some degree of experience with marriage. Black singles are the least likely to reject the holiness of the Son of God by asserting that He sinned: 38% buy this view, compared to 47% of white singles, and 53% of Hispanic singles. Unmarried people living in the Northeast are also particularly prone to this view (53%). Amazingly, 30% of born again singles believe that Jesus sinned.

In like manner, more than four out of ten single people (43%) say that Jesus died but never had a physical resurrection, as claimed in the Bible. Some would submit that perhaps He had a spiritual resurrection, but not a bodily return from the dead after three days.

The perceived existence of Jesus is placed in context by the revelation that only half of the never-been-married segment, two-thirds of the widowed contingent, and seven out of ten divorced people strongly affirm, "Jesus Christ is alive today." While less than one out of ten singles believe strongly that He does not live, a large proportion fall in the gray zone of leaning one way or the other, but not having a certainty about the matter.

Views on other supernatural beings seem no less confused. For instance, more than four out of ten singles strongly agree, "The Holy Spirit is not a living being but is simply a symbol of God's power or presence." In fact, two-thirds of all singles maintain some level of agreement with this idea; only one out of every five singles strongly denies that the Holy Spirit is merely symbolic. Astoundingly, born again singles are no different than their unsaved counterparts on the existence of the Holy Spirit.

Americans, including most single adults, generally dismiss the existence of Satan. Four out of ten single adults strongly agree that Satan is merely a symbol of evil rather than a living being; two out of three singles agree to some extent with that view. Less than one out of four single adults firmly resist the idea that Satan is symbolic. Once again, shockingly little difference exists between single Christian and single non-Christians on this matter.

The Bible Belt Lives On

One of the enduring cultural realities of the U.S. is the existence of the "Bible belt." Although virtually everything related to traditional spiritual practices and institutions has taken a beating in the past half century – and the Bible Belt has not escaped the influence of paganism and postmodernism – the Southern states remain notably different in spiritual climate and practice. Single adults in the South are becoming more like the "typical" adult throughout the nation, but at a slower rate of change. Generally, the people in the Northeast and West have moved the farthest from biblical views, people in the South are the most likely to hold biblical views, and folks in the Midwest sit somewhere in-between the extremes.

You can witness this pattern throughout the data, as evident in the accompanying table. Single adults in the Northeast and West are the *least likely* to describe themselves as Christian, to strongly assert that the Bible is accurate, to firmly contend that they have a personal responsibility to evangelize, to reject the notion that Jesus sinned, to possess a biblical understanding of God's nature, to claim that their faith is very important to them, and to fit the born again criteria. They are the most likely to strongly affirm that a good person can earn eternal salvation.

What Single Adults Believe, by Region[4]

perspective	NE	SOU	MW	WST
religious faith they consider themselves to be:				
Christian	76%	88%	84%	77%
non-Christian faith	10	5	6	9
atheist/agnostic	10	4	7	12
the Bible is totally accurate in all of its teachings				
agree strongly	29	47	36	31
disagree strongly	23	13	18	23
personally have a responsibility to tell other people your religious beliefs				
agree strongly	20	37	29	24
disagree strongly	37	21	30	37
your religious faith is very important in your life				
agree strongly	57	73	62	59
disagree strongly	9	4	5	9
the devil, or Satan, is not a living being but is simply a symbol of evil				
agree strongly	44	43	40	38
disagree strongly	20	25	20	26
if a person is generally good, or does enough good things for others during their life, they will earn a place in Heaven				
agree strongly	38	31	31	35
disagree strongly	20	29	25	23
when He lived on earth, Jesus Christ was human and committed sins, like other people				
agree strongly	27	24	24	25
disagree strongly	30	41	39	32
God is the all-powerful, all-knowing Creator of the universe who still rules the world today	60	74	65	57
born again Christian (made personal commitment to Christ that's still important, and believe they will go to Heaven because they confessed their sins and accepted Christ as their savior)	23	46	36	30

Key: NE=North East; SOU=South; MW=Mid-West; WST=West

On the other hand, single adults living in the South remain the ***most likely*** to describe themselves as Christian, to strongly assert that the Bible is accurate, to firmly contend that they have a personal responsibility to evangelize, to describe their faith as very important in their life, to reject the notion that Jesus sinned, to maintain a biblical understanding of God's nature, and to meet the survey definition of "born again." Southern singles are the most likely to dismiss the notion that a good person can earn eternal salvation.

Over the next few decades, the regional distinctions that we see today are likely to virtually disappear. One major reason is the transience of our population. With one out of every six households changing location each year, and young adults demonstrating an even higher rate of mobility than was evident in the past, there will be a heightened mixing of backgrounds. Add to that the homogenization of the nation's churches, the virtual absence of spiritual training within the family unit, and the increasing impact of the mass media upon people's spiritual inclinations, and we have great reason to expect the elimination of regional differences in the not-too-distant future.

Footnotes

[1] These figures come from an analysis of eight national quarterly tracking studies undertaken by the Barna Research Group, involving 8049 adults, of whom 3817 were single adults: 3695 who have never been married, 1051 who were widowed, and 1638 divorced individuals. These studies were fielded via telephone with random samples of adults once every three months, from January 2000 through November 2001.

[2] It is important to keep in mind that only God knows the true heart of people, and thus only He knows if a person is truly born again in His Son. Our research is not an attempt to judge people, but to estimate what seems to be happening in our culture with regard to salvation and personal relationships with Jesus. I use the term "born again Christian" to describe those who say they have made a personal commitment to Jesus that remains important to them and who expect to inhabit Heaven because of their acknowledgment of their sins, asking for God's forgiveness and reliance upon Christ as their savior in order to differentiate this group from the multitudes who call themselves "Christian" but have no such basis for their faith and hope for eternity.

[3] Based on one or more national surveys of random samples of 1000 or more adults, conducted by the Barna Research Group, from January 2000 through November 2001.

[4] Based on one or more national surveys of random samples of 1000 or more adults, conducted by the Barna Research Group, from January 2000 through November 2001.

Chapter 8
ARE CHRISTIAN SINGLES DIFFERENT?

Christianity is not meant to be merely a series of religious exercises that change our schedules but not our hearts. The Christian faith is meant to be life transforming, causing us to be more like Jesus Christ. Such change should be evident in every dimension of our lives – our emotional, interpersonal, intellectual, financial, vocational, and recreational as well as spiritual condition. In God's economy, no room exists for shallow faith: we either sell out to His way of life or to the world's, but there is no in-between haven for the complacent or weak to hide within. Yet, having said that, this transformation is a lifelong process that will never be complete until those who embrace Jesus Christ as their Lord and Savior are reunited with Him in heaven. We are called to be obedient, but not expected to be perfect.

How are unmarried Christians doing in that spiritually-driven life transition? It's not an easy factor to assess. One means of evaluating the state of the Christian singles population is to compare their standing on a variety of factors to that of single non-believers. (Throughout this chapter, as I have in this entire book, I will be defining "Christian" singles as those who meet the "born again" criteria we use in our surveys: they say they have made a "personal commitment to Jesus Christ that is still important in my life today" and believe they will have eternal life with God in heaven only because they have confessed their sins and accepted Christ as their savior.)

Living Like A Believer

The most overt – and definitive – way to discern an individual's commitment to Christ is by observing the manner in which they live. Many dimensions comprise our daily experience, and each is susceptible to change once we choose to imitate the life and values of Jesus. Let's briefly explore how Christian singles view themselves regarding seven areas of self-perception.

While Christian singles are slightly less likely to describe themselves as "too busy" (40% do so, versus 47% of non-Christian singles), they are no less likely to describe themselves as "stressed out." One-third of single adults who have accepted Christ admit that they feel overwhelmed by anxieties and pressures. Part of this feeling of helplessness is un-doubtedly related to the fact that about half of all single adults, regardless of their faith commitment, say they are still searching for the meaning and purpose of their life. The absence of such insight invariably produces unnecessary and confounding stress on a regular basis.

It is curious that Christians would continue to struggle with the meaning and purpose of their life. There are two ways in which people might address this issue: identifying their mission (i.e., the general purpose of being alive), and God's vision for their life (i.e., a specific and compelling mental portrait of a preferable future that God has called them to pursue).

Understanding mission is the first – and easiest – step, since it is the most general and generic. All believers are called to the same mission, which may be communicated in various ways, but essentially relates to obeying Luke 10:27 – to love God with all of our heart, mind, strength and soul, and loving our neighbors as we love ourselves. Describing mission in terms that the individual resonates with is important, but possessing an understanding of what mission is and how it, alone, can direct one's life is a necessary and elementary step for believers. It appears that few of them have a grasp of the nature and significance of declaring their life's mission.

Vision conveys a deeper level of understanding of our uniqueness in Christ and His special expectation and calling to us. As our research into the process of understanding and implementing God's vision has shown us, this is something that takes greater time, effort, study and commitment.[1] However, it is also one of the character traits of individual's who ultimately make great in-roads for the kingdom in their own sphere of life. Enabling people to distinguish between their personal vision (human-driven) and God's vision (Spirit and Bible-driven) is important in this maturation and clarification process.

The fact that half of all believers say they are searching for meaning and purpose suggests that they have yet to understand God's mission for their life. That is a shortcoming that we, as friends or leaders whom they trust, can help them overcome.

131

Surprisingly few singles say that their career comes first in their life, and Christian singles are no more (or less) likely than others to make such a claim. Christians singles are, however, notably less likely to indicate that they like to try new experiences (70% versus 85%, respectively). While most singles like trying new things, fewer Christians possess the adventurous spirit of non-believers.

One of the great pressure points in the lives of singles relates to finances. Christian singles were indistinguishable from their non-Christian counterparts in this area of life, which may also help explain the identical stress levels of both segments. Our research shows that single adults are equally likely to say they are struggling financially, in debt, and living comfortably, regardless of their spiritual orientation and commitments.

The personal relationships of believers look very similar in some ways to those of non-believers. Although they are slightly more likely to describe themselves as "very relational," Christian singles are every bit as likely as non-believers to be actively searching for a few good friends, to engage in similar types of conversations with others, and to prefer being in control of situations they encounter. Believers are more likely to try to avoid conflict with others and are less likely to be willing to make tough decisions. These two related perspectives suggest that many Christians may inadvertently disqualify themselves from leadership positions because they are more likely to shy away from the challenging situations that test and define leaders.

In addition to appreciating control, most singles, regardless of their faith orientation, see themselves as self-sufficient – and tend to behave accordingly. No difference exists between the two segments in terms of their concern about the future, although the September 11 terrorist attacks did raise the level of concern among the non-Christians a bit.

One of the biggest differences relates to the sociopolitical ideology of the two groups. Christians are more likely to view themselves as mostly conservative (33%) than mostly liberal (10%), while non-Christian singles are slightly more likely to see themselves as liberal rather than conservative. Keep in mind, however, that a majority of all singles see themselves as being somewhere in the middle: half of all Christian singles and six out of ten non-Christian singles say they are "somewhere in-between" the ends of the ideological continuum.

The area of self-image in which believers and non-believers have the most substantial differences relates to spirituality. Six out of ten unmarried singles say they are "spiritual," compared to nine out of ten born again singles. When we tightened the self-definition a bit and asked if they see themselves as "deeply spiritual," the numbers shrank accordingly: eight out of ten believers embraced the label, compared to only half of the non-believers.

One of the more intriguing outcomes was discovering that only two-thirds of the singles who fit the survey classification of "born again" actually accept that term to describe themselves. At the same time, one-fifth of those who do not meet the survey criteria for "born again" think of themselves as being a born again Christian. Although only God truly knows who is and is not a disciple of Jesus, these research-based estimates suggest that we have to be careful about labels and stereotypes – even those that people adopt for themselves. A single adult who considers himself to be born again may not have the type of relationship with Christ that does, in fact, incorporate them into the true Church, while a single who does not use such a description may nevertheless have exactly the type of faith and life commitment that honors the Lord – and qualifies them for such an esteemed title.

Even beyond self-image, though, the research shows that single adults have other similarities and differences from peers who do not share their faith orientation. One such dimension is in the area of music. While all singles, regardless of spiritual leanings, are equally likely to purchase recordings throughout the year, the two groups prefer divergent types of music.

The three most widely appreciated musical styles of born again singles are Christian, R&B and country, each named by more than 10% as their favorite genre. The least appreciated styles are country, rock and rap/hip-hop, also each mentioned by at least 10% as their least favored genres. When we compare the proportions of singles who like a genre and subtract the percentage who dislike the genre, a different picture emerges, one that portrays the types of music that people are most comfortable hearing. Those styles are Christian, R&B, pop, jazz and alternative (primarily among unmarried singles).

The profile is somewhat different among the non-Christian singles. The preferred styles are rock and country. The most disliked styles are rap/hip-hop, country and rock. In other words, there is substantial heterogeneity among non-Christian singles. The net preference list includes R&B, jazz, pop, Christian and alternative.

One of the most significant insights this analysis brings to the table, though, is how splintered the singles market looks in terms of musical preferences. Because music is the single, most powerful language in our culture today, it is important to provide people the sound with which they resonate. Doing so makes the statement that the ministry is sensitive to, and in touch with the needs and desires of the target audience. But clearly, the sound that attracts one group of singles will repulse another group. While R&B and Christian may be the "safest" sounds to employ in a ministry setting, they are also styles that will fail to move a large proportion of the unmarried mass.

Musical Preferences of Single Adults, by Faith Orientation[2]

musical style	born again singles			non-born again singles		
	favorite	dislike	net acceptance	favorite	dislike	net acceptance
Christian	24%	1%	+23 points	4%	2%	+ 2 points
R&B	14	*	+14	8	1	+ 7
pop	6	1	+ 5	6	3	+ 3
jazz	6	2	+ 4	6	1	+ 5
alternative/grunge	4	*	+ 4	2	*	+ 2
country	12	17	- 5	11	18	- 7
heavy metal	*	8	- 8	*	9	- 9
rock	9	20	-11	19	11	+ 8
rap, hip-hop	3	33	-30	7	35	-28

Sociopolitical realities are yet another area of differentiation. Not only are born again singles twice as likely to be mostly conservative, and only half as likely to be mostly liberal, but born again singles are also more likely to be registered to vote, more likely to be Republican and less likely to be independent, and more likely to have voted for George Bush than Al Gore in the hotly-contested 2000 presidential election. (Born again singles gave Bush a small margin over Gore; non-born again singles, on the other hand, supported Gore by a 2-to-1 margin.)

One of the significant determinants of people's lifestyle, i.e., technology, is generally similar between singles who are believers and those who are not. Levels of ownership of electronic equipment were virtually identical, and the ways in which the two niches use the Internet differed only slightly. Christian singles were somewhat more likely to use the Net for faith-related experiences and for video games, and somewhat less likely to keep up existing relationships through e-mail and online discussions. Overall, electronics are owned and used just as often – and deployed for the same reasons and in same ways – by singles, no matter where they stand with Jesus Christ.

Thinking Like A Believer

The goals that singles have set for themselves are significantly flavored by one's religious inklings. There are certain life outcomes that both segments share an interest in experiencing, such as good health, clarity of life purpose and living with integrity. But there are some huge gaps between the groups, as well.

Christian singles were more likely to prioritize having a close personal relationship with God (ranked first among the 21 possible alternatives, compared to a ninth-place finish among non-born agains), being deeply committed to the Christian faith (rated fifth by Christians, 15th by non-Christians), and being active in a local church (rated eighth, compared to 19th among the non-believers). Notice that the dimensions that Christians rated more highly dealt with faith.

Non-Christian singles were much more likely to prioritize close friend-ships (their second-ranked goal, which was ranked sixth by believers), a comfortable lifestyle (third highest, compared to a 10th-place finish among believers), and having satisfying sex with their marriage partner (seventh on the list, but just 13th among believers). These factors relate to comfort and security, which the Christian singles may be expecting to receive to a greater degree through their faith commitments.

The area in which faith leanings make the greatest difference relates to moral perspectives. Christian singles have significantly different views from non-Christian singles in relation to 15 of the 20 areas of moral and ethical living that we studied. In fact, there are 12 areas in which the moral views of the two niches differ by more than twenty percentage points, which is the level at which the differences become practically significant rather than merely statistically significant. The information shows that Christian singles are most likely to have different moral standards on issues such as abortion, homosexuality, cohabitation, sexual infidelity, pornography and drunkenness.

Also worth noting, however, are some moral issues on which Christian singles have a divergent perspective from that of non-Christian singles, and yet less than half of Christian singles maintain a conservative view on the matter. For instance, only four out of ten Christians contend that there are moral absolutes – higher than the three out of ten among non-Christians, but still a relatively low percentage. The Matthew 5 idea that divorce is a sin unless it is a response to marital infidelity is accepted by only one-third of the Christian singles – twice the proportion of nonbelievers, but still comparatively depressed. In like manner, it is disturbing to note that only half of Christian singles consider cohabitation to be morally unacceptable and that just half say that sexual fantasies are inappropriate.

Differences In Moral Perspectives of Singles,
by Their Faith Commitment[3]

moral perspective	born again	not born again
there are moral absolutes that are unchanging	43%	29%
abortion should be illegal in all or most circumstances	63	38
homosexuality should be legal between consenting adults	42	65
approve of clergy performing/blessing gay marriages	19	46
except when related to adultery, divorce is a sin	35	18
cohabitation is morally acceptable	47	79
marijuana use for non-medicinal purposes is morally acceptable	10	39
having sexual relations with a person of same sex is morally acceptable	10	42
watching a movie with explicit sex or nudity is morally acceptable	34	66
reading a magazine with explicit sexual pictures or nudity is morally acceptable	26	65
using profanity is morally acceptable	28	52
getting drunk is morally acceptable	22	50
having an abortion is morally acceptable	23	53
speeding is morally acceptable	35	48
having sexual thoughts or fantasies is morally acceptable	48	76

Christian singles also have some areas of moral and ethical perspective in which they are indistinguishable from their non-Christian peers. Among those are elements such as the basis of their moral decision-making. Although you might expect Christian singles to rely more heavily upon influences such as the Bible or religious teaching, we found that this was not the case. Other dimensions of moral behavior on which the thoughts of Christian and non-Christian singles were a mirror image included having an affair with an unmarried person, keeping excess change knowingly received by mistake, and lying on a resume to increase one's chances of securing a desirable job.

Moral Perspectives That Are Similar Among
Both Christian and Non-Christian Singles[4]

moral perspective	born again	not born again
the basis of your moral/ethical decisions is:		
the Bible	17%	12%
values taught by your parents	13	12
whatever feels right or comfortable in the situation	24	26
whatever produces the best personal outcome	13	14
having an affair with an unmarried person is morally acceptable	21	28
keeping excess change given to you by mistake is morally acceptable	15	19
lying on a resume about your education or job achievements is morally acceptable	10	11

Believing Like A Believer

Just as believers and non-believers have different views on many moral issues, so do they possess a variety of divergent theological perspectives. Keep in mind that one of the key theological differences relates to whether or not they are born again – and that only one out of every three singles is born again. Also remember that just one out of every seven born again singles is an evangelical – meaning that they are not only born again but also believe that the Bible is accurate, that they have a responsibility to share their faith with non-believers, that Satan is real, Jesus was holy, salvation cannot be earned, and God is the holy, omnipotent and omniscient creator and ruler of all things. The fact that so few people who trust Christ for their salvation fail to believe this handful of core biblical truths is a revealing commentary on the state of the Church today – and on the spiritual depth of single adults.

From a macro-level vantage point, note that most people, whether they know Jesus intimately or not, think of themselves as Christian. Three out of four non-born again singles use that name. Also most of today's single adults were churched while growing up, something that will change with the emerging generations (i.e., the Mosaics), but 83% of the born again and 57% of non-born again singles were church-goers when they were young. Little that we do in church will surprise most singles, and a large share of them (more than three-quarters) think they already know all the core beliefs of the Christian faith and therefore have little to learn.

The specific beliefs of the two segments diverge, however, on most theological matters that go beyond simplistic concepts. Christians are three times more likely to strongly contend that the Bible is accurate in its teachings, to assert that they have a duty to share their faith, and to strongly disagree that a good person can earn salvation. They are twice as likely as non-believers to describe themselves as "absolutely committed" to Christianity, and to firmly believe that God created the universe and that Jesus is alive today. They are twice as likely as non-believers to strongly disagree that all of the major faith groups teach the same lessons, that Jesus never had a physical resurrection, that Jesus committed sins, that Satan is symbolic but not real and that the Holy Spirit is symbolic but not real. Believers were also notably more likely to assert that their faith is very important in their life, that God gave us free will which therefore allows us to choose our eternal destiny, and they are much more likely to reject the idea that there are some sins that God cannot forgive. Even on a simple matter such as perceptions of the nature of God, born again singles were very different: nine out of ten endorsed the view of God as the all-knowing, all-powerful Creator, while only half of the non-believers accept that view.

While the single adults who follow Christ are notably different than other singles in their religious views, it is also useful to see ample room for growth in their theological maturity. For instance, only one-third of Christian singles strongly reject the idea that Satan doesn't exist but is merely symbolic. Less than half of all believers firmly believes that salvation cannot be earned – an amazing statistic given that all of these individuals are personally relying on grace rather than good deeds as their means to eternal security. Less than one-third strongly disagrees that the Holy Spirit does not exist, which also raises some devastating theological consequences. Barely half of all single believers strongly disagrees that Jesus never had a physical resurrection, again raising serious questions about either the biblical knowledge or the depth of confidence in Scripture that these people possess.

What Christian and Non-Christian Singles Believe[5]

perspective		born again	not born again
the Bible is totally accurate in all of its teachings			
	agree strongly	62%	23%
	disagree strongly	5	26
personally have a responsibility to tell other people your religious beliefs			
	agree strongly	49	17
	disagree strongly	12	40
your religious faith is very important in your life			
	agree strongly	87	51
	disagree strongly	1	10
the devil, or Satan, is not a living being but is simply a symbol of evil			
	agree strongly	39	43
	disagree strongly	36	16
if a person is generally good, or does enough good things for others during their life, they will earn a place in Heaven			
	agree strongly	22	40
	disagree strongly	44	15
when He lived on earth, Jesus Christ was human and committed sins, like other people			
	agree strongly	18	29
	disagree strongly	58	24
the Holy Spirit is a symbol of God's presence or power but is not a living entity			
	agree strongly	46	43
	disagree strongly	31	12
God is the all-powerful, all-knowing Creator of the universe who still rules the world today		89	52

When we quizzed people about the importance of each of eight key religious activities, non-believers were less likely to rate each of these as "very important" than were believers. While more than half of the believers described each of the eight endeavors as very important, only two of those practices reached that level of significance among non-believers (i.e., worshiping God and learning about their faith). Fellowship, stewardship, evangelism, serving the needy and accountability were all deemed to be of great importance to half or less of the non-Christian singles population.

Non-Christian singles are generally leery of getting too deeply involved or invested in personal spiritual development. Just one-third had standards they use to evaluate their spiritual condition – a statistic that was identical to that of Christian singles – and they were slightly less likely than the believers to follow ideas provided to them by leaders and disciplers who would take them under their wing and strive to help them grow in Christ. This may be due to fear of the unknown. When they were asked to describe the content of personal spiritual growth, the non-Christian singles were three times more likely than believers to say they had no idea what that might entail or the product they would seek.

Are Christian Singles Different?

Clearly, Christian singles are in a different place spiritually and morally than are non-believers – which is good for the Church. This provides the Church with a contingent of disciples who can reasonably be expected to share their faith with non-Christians and to help those individuals mature in their faith.

The statistics underscore the importance of realizing that when we have the opportunity to interact with non-Christian single adults, they are coming from a different point-of-view on many aspects of life, ranging from values and morals to beliefs and relationships. Ministry to groups is difficult in this regard unless the group is truly homogeneous – which, in turn, suggests that perhaps we have not done an adequate job of reaching out to the majority who do not know Christ and who do not have much to do with churches. If we are attracting single adults to activities at the church, we have to remember that they view the world through a different set of lenses, and we must tailor our interaction with them accordingly – never compromising the gospel and its implications, but always contextualizing those elements so that the uninitiated can understand what we are saying, embrace it and then follow it.

Footnotes

[1] For a deeper discussion of this process, see my book on understanding, identifying, articulating and pursuing God's vision in life, *Turning Vision Into Action* (Regal Books: Ventura, CA, 1994).

[2] Based on a national survey of 1017 randomly selected adults, conducted by the Barna Research Group, October 2000.

[3] Based on a national survey of 1003 randomly selected adults, including 491 singles, conducted by the Barna Research Group, May 2001.

[4] Based on a national survey of 1017 randomly selected adults, conducted by the Barna Research Group, October 2000.

[5] Based on one or more national surveys of random samples of 1000 or more adults, conducted by the Barna Research Group, from January 2000 through November 2001.

Chapter 9
MAKING THE MOST OF MINISTRY TO SINGLES

Now that the evidence has been presented, would you agree that there are very distinct singles populations that require special attention and unique response if we are to know, love and serve them appropriately? Whether you interact with single adults at work, in the neighborhood, through leisure pursuits, within your family, or in a ministry context, addressing their unique needs, preferences, expectations and life approaches demands that we have an accurate knowledge of where they're coming from and where they're going. Like most Americans, single adults generally want to be known and loved, accepted for who they are and helped in areas in which they are weak. You and I have a tremendous opportunity to be agents of influence and transformation in the lives of unmarried people if we adequately understand what makes them tick, and what we can do to facilitate their maturation.

Let me summarize some of the conclusions I've drawn from this body of information. First, let's consider what we need to know about all singles groups, then we'll consider some of the idiosyncrasies of each of the three major singles niches. You may have drawn entirely different conclusions or developed different priorities based on the information presented so far – and that's great! My motivation is to provide a summary interpretation and exhortation for you to ponder. The bottom line, though, is for you to be so confident that you have something to offer to single adults, and to become so intentional and strategic in how you choose to reach out to those people, that you will act with vigor, wisdom and faith. Nothing is worse than understanding without action! No matter what conclusions you have drawn, commit yourself to putting your insights and ideas into play.

What All Single Adults Need

One of the striking realities about America's unmarried population is that just one-third has accepted Jesus Christ as their savior. Increasing that percentage needs to be a priority for the church – but what will it take?

At the risk of sounding simplistic, single adults who do not know the saving love of Christ need our prayers. Can you become an intercessor for one single adult? Can you recruit other prayer partners to adopt other unsaved single adults and pray them toward the cross? Focused, sincere prayer from godly people changes the world. You can become part of a moral and spiritual revolution by praying without ceasing for the souls of specific people. Find a single adult who is seeking to make it from day to day without Christ dwelling in their heart, and pray them into the kingdom!

If you are able to engage in a more interactive approach, consider how you might get singles to truly engage with God's Word. Singles are lukewarm toward the Bible. Their refusal to read it consistently, to take its content at face value, and to translate its substance into a worldview based on truth has undermined their capacity to know and emulate Christ. Confounding the situation is their belief that they already know what the Bible has to say and their stated intention not to alter their views about what they think the Bible teaches. In reality, young singles remain largely ignorant of its principles, while older singles appear to be anesthetized to its truths.

For some singles, a valuable first step would be to obtain a version of the Scriptures that they can more readily understand. Most unmarried adults need help in becoming reacquainted with the Bible through creative introductions to the content – getting beyond the basic stories they have heard since childhood – and providing personally meaningful applications. All of this must be done purposefully, however, which demands study and teaching that leads somewhere big – that is, to a coherent, comprehensive, compelling worldview. The last thing single adults need is a tidbit of truth here and an interesting idea there. For decades, they have had exposure to elements of truth, but without having the dots connected to display God's grand philosophy. Although they cannot articulate the need, singles are desperately seeking the revelation of that grand design – not just the means to salvation, but the mosaic of wisdom that reveals God's greater purposes and interwoven truth. Until these things are shown to singles in clear and unmistakable ways, they will continue their fruitless search for meaning, purpose and fulfillment with frustration.

Once they achieve such an appreciation for the Bible, and get a grip on God's unchanging truths, it will be possible for them to concentrate on deepening their spiritual maturity by intelligently and passionately focusing on the pillars of the faith. While most singles have an area or two of faith that they truly embrace as significant, it is that lopsided, incomplete perspective on Christianity that enables them to be so lukewarm about following Christ. Helping singles to understand the identity and significance of the pillars, and to realistically evaluate where they stand in relation to the six focal points of the faith would constitute a major leap forward toward becoming stellar believers.[1]

Ultimately, of course, these new insights and perspectives should impact their values and resulting lifestyle choices. That is one benefit of having a godly worldview: it serves as the filter through which every choice is made and every decision is evaluated. Upon observing how single adults live – especially those who claim to be followers of Jesus – if the evidence does not support their claim to being a disciple, then those who serve the Church must hold our unmarried peers accountable for their choices and behaviors. This is true for never-been-marrieds, divorced and widowed adults: few of them have biblical standards and loving accountability enforced by caring Christian peers integrated into their daily efforts.

Critical elements in our ability to help single adults grow, however, are our commitment to a genuine relationship with them and our ability to model an authentic Christian life. Like most people, singles shield themselves from the influence of those whom they do not know and trust. They are most open to ideas and constructive criticism from people with whom they have developed a true bond. Outsiders who engage in "hit and run discipleship" – that is, criticizing others without having first established credibility through relationship – often do more damage than benefit for the kingdom through their well-intentioned but reckless

148

approach. To gain a hearing and serious consideration from singles, show your real concern for who they are by taking the time and making the effort to engage them in a true friendship.

At the same time, friends undermine the credibility of their words if their behavior does not demonstrate the truths they profess and the expectations they convey of others. Millions of Americans, single as well as married, distance themselves from the Church and the ways of Christ because of the overt hypocrisy of alleged believers. Few Americans – especially those who are likely to reject the existence of absolute morality and the purity of the Christian faith – winningly pursue a faith that seems inherently impossible to live or innately flawed on the basis of how it is portrayed by its followers. The individuals who make inroads for Christ in the lives of others are those believers who not only demonstrate the love of Christ by investing themselves in significant relationships but who also pursue and reflect the life principles of Jesus in their personal behavior.

What Never-Been-Marrieds Need

To impact the lives of those who have never ventured into marriage, keep in mind what turns their crank: satisfying relationships, group activities, interesting adventures, authenticity, efforts that build or reinforce their self-esteem, and opportunities to succeed. The more you are able to incorporate an understanding of these needs into your interactions with them, the more trusted and relied upon you will become – and the greater your opportunity for influence.

Because they tend to be younger adults, and are therefore still feeling their way through the process of becoming established in the workplace and within a network of supportive relationships, offering options that educate while facilitating meaningful interaction will be welcomed. Taking the time to truly listen, and to provide a process of discovery rather than a standard package of indisputable answers, fits their need. Using media, music and language that reflect their background and expectations is beneficial as you attempt to gain their attention and consideration. Eschewing the goal of building "the biggest singles ministry in town" in favor of creating an environment in which they experience energy, value, acceptance, purpose and hope more often than not produces sincere involvement and significant personal growth.

Few never-been-marrieds have a significant understanding of the spiritual pillars – although they would resent such a statement. As simplistic as it may seem, you will need to introduce them to what it means to experience the presence of God in worship; how to develop and implement a biblical worldview; why personal brokenness and an urgency about forgiveness and holiness are needed, and how to get there; what holistic stewardship means, and holding them accountable for practicing it; why serving the needy is imperative, and how to get involved in such service; and the way to develop biblical community. If this seems like a Basic Christian Foundations exercise, that's exactly what it is – because that's precisely what they have missed out on all of their lives.

What Widowed Adults Need

Widowed adults live life at quite a different pace – and that's the way they prefer it to stay. They have paid their dues and seen it all, and most widowed adults want to enjoy a peaceful existence during whatever years they have left. They do not want more responsibility, nor control, nor conflict. They are happy to help a ministry but they don't want to shoulder its burdens. They are more comfortable with predictable routines than exciting surprises. The ministry that understands this mindset and strategically works within its boundaries will thrive.

Although most widowed adults are more spiritually mature than the average single adult, and are more interested in pursuing matters of faith, they have weak points. They attend church services as their health allows, and they feel attendance is in itself a statement, but surprisingly few of them really understand the reality of experiencing God's presence and interacting with His Spirit in a personal and worshipful way. Helping them to gain a deeper understanding of worship will open up new vistas on life for the widowed.

A portion of the widowed population will respond to the opportunity to mentor a younger person, as long as it can be done in their own style. Don't expect written plans, extensive reading lists and rigorous assessments; they are more likely to recount some of the lessons they have learned over their years of seeking and knowing God. The youngest two generations – the Mosaics and the Busters – are most likely to resonate with who widowed folks are and their style of interaction. Facilitating those opportunities would be valuable for both parties.

Generally genial and relational, widowed people want social opportunities without pressure to participate. They want to be known and cared for, but not to be relied upon for production. Because most widowed people are elderly women, one of the consistent needs expressed is for peers in the faith to keep an eye on their health care and housing situations. They expect their church to demonstrate an interest in their welfare and to lend a hand in tying loose ends together when they need assistance.

What Divorced Adults Need

Life is a wild seesaw ride for many divorced adults. Their standard state of being is to feel physically fatigued, emotionally drained, financially strapped and spiritually confused. They generally wallow in uncertainty about getting remarried and maintaining viable relationships with their children (if they had any) from their former marriage. These are people who are stressed and need maximum space and understanding. They will be irritating sometimes because they want control, but that is merely a product of their insecurity, distrust and hectic lives.

Don't expect most divorced adults to get real excited about church involvement. There is a great level of fear of rejection and abandonment – again – by other Christians due to their divorce. Consequently, their spirituality is often a very meaningful but private affair. Persuading them to engage in corporate spiritual life will take time, sensitivity and perceived benefits. They have no time to waste and no energy to spare: make it great or get out of their way.

Many divorced people retain a level of anger with God – "How could He let this happen to me?" – that does not subside for years, if ever. When it comes to their faith, they want to make it real and central to their lives, but only if they can see the benefit and work it around all the imperatives in their pressure-packed lives. Chances are good they don't really understand worship, and they have only a passing knowledge of the Bible, and that they have no time for community service efforts and cannot afford to return God's resources as a good steward would. In other words, they will view their circumstances as a viable excuse for not engaging with God in as deep a way as they need to. Coaching them into a slowly growing commitment is your best bet.

Are They Worth It?

If you are developing a ministry to single adults through your church, you might consider the value of a "stealth singles ministry," that is, a ministry that focuses on helping single adults, but outside the boundaries of the typical "singles ghetto." More and more we are hearing from singles that they do not want to live outside the mainstream of the congregation simply because they are not married: they want to be completey bonded to the heartbeat of the church and get their singles fix in some other way. Ministries that are able to mainstream singles often provide a personal touch through events designed to aid singles and through developing relational networks that meet their unique needs.

Now that you know many of the complexities of singles, and can see just how challenging such a ministry might be, are you asking whether ministry to single adults is worth the effort? (If you're not, I suspect you're not paying attention!) In arriving at an answer, consider these two thoughts.

First, God loves all His people. He does not discriminate on the basis of their marital status. (In fact, some would make the argument that Paul's admonition to stay single, if possible, suggests that God recognizes the benefits of remaining single.) Singles are precious to Him – He dearly loves them and, therefore, so should we.

Second, if the Bible is meant to direct and shape our thoughts about ministry, then keep in mind that more than a few of the greatest leaders and examples in Scripture were single. These patrons of our faith demonstrate the dramatic impact an unmarried person can have upon the world. From Ruth and Mary, from John the Baptist to Paul – and even Jesus – the Bible underscores the significant contributions of singles. It is our privilege to know and love and serve them. It is my prayer that through this book, you are now blessed with additional knowledge that will make that task easier and more fulfilling.

Footnotes

[1] One of the diagnostic tools we have developed is the Personal Spiritual Inventory, a simple and quick way of determining where a person stands in regard to the pillars. For more information about this self-administered inventory, consult the Barna Research Group website, at www.barna.org.

APPENDIX

RESEARCH
METHODOLOGY

This book is based on data derived from eight nationwide surveys among adults conducted by the Barna Research Group, Ltd. of Ventura, California. In each survey a random sample of adults was drawn from the 48 continental states and a survey questionnaire was administered to individuals. These telephone surveys were conducted from the Barna Research field facility in Ventura. The timing and related statistics pertaining to those surveys are shown below:

		sample size	
OmniPoll™	dates conducted	total	singles
OP 1-00	January 2000	1002	469
OP S-00	April 2000	1003	458
OP 2-00	July 2000	1008	446
OP F-00	November 2000	1017	479
OP 1-01	January 2001	1005	504
OP S-01	April 2001	1003	491
OP 2-01	August 2001	1001	496
OP F-01	November 2001	1010	474

The surveys were conducted through the use of the random-digit dial (RDD) sampling technique. In this method we derive a representative nationwide sample of telephone numbers that have been randomly generated. We then call the household and screen respondents to determine whether or not a qualified person lives in the home. If so, we attempt to conduct the interview with them. While we are not able to connect with every eligible adult whose home we call, our response rates in qualified households exceed industry norms. In these surveys, the response rates averaged 71% in the qualified households. The average survey lasted anywhere from 16 to 21 minutes per respondent. The maximum amount of sampling error associated with the aggregate survey is plus or minus three percentage points at the 95% confidence level. The maximum sampling error associated with the singles subgroups is approximately plus or minus five percentage points.

ABOUT THE BARNA RESEARCH GROUP, LTD.

BARNA
*Research
Group, LTD*

The Barna Research Group (BRG) was initiated in 1984 by George and Nancy Barna to serve the information needs of the Church. BRG's vision is "to provide Christian ministries with current, accurate and reliable information, in bite-sized pieces, at reasonable cost, to help them to be more strategic in their decision-making." The company has been honored to serve thousands of ministries since its inception.

Barna Research helps ministries by:

  • offering a wealth of free, current information on-line, through the BRG web site (www.barna.org) and the bi-weekly publication of its latest findings

  • conducting primary research related to specific information, development and marketing needs of an organization

  • providing resources – books, reports, videos, audiotapes, newsletters – that describe BRG's research and how the findings apply to ministry

  • conducting intensive classes and seminars for church leaders, revealing insights from primary research conducted for the seminar

- presenting information in conferences, seminars and other meetings
- providing research-based consultation related to articulated ministry needs.

BRG uses both quantitative and qualitative research methods to generate relevant and reliable information that reveals insights to enhance ministry efforts. Among the types of research commonly conducted by BRG are:

- attitudinal and behavioral surveys of congregations
- lifestyle, values, behavior and beliefs profiles of communities
- profiles of the attitudes, expectations, giving habits and needs of donors
- evaluations of new products: perceived value, pricing, marketing, etc.
- name recognition and ministry image studies
- employee perception studies
- efficiency and effectiveness studies
- product use studies
- customer service and customer satisfaction
- segmentation studies to identify tapped and untapped potential
- media use surveys

If you would like to know more about Barna Research, please explore our web site. If you are interested in conducting primary research to solve some of your ministry and marketing challenges, call us at 1-800-55-BARNA. For further information, visit the Barna Research Group, Ltd. web site at www.barna.org.

TAKING ADVANTAGE OF BARNA RESEARCH

Because we are committed to helping the Church live up to its God-given calling, we try to support ministries with strategic information. While the books and reports we develop contain much of the data and related interpretation, we have also created a web site geared to arming ministers – lay and professional – with the strategic intelligence they need to make great decisions in ministry. Here are suggestions on using our services:

1.   **Visit our web site: www.barna.org.** Explore the various pages on the site to discover what we have to offer. Although you may not need it all today, it might be useful in the future.

2.   **Subscribe to our free e-publication, The Barna Update, which is available only through the web site.** Every two weeks or so George Barna releases a new report based upon the most recent information from Barna Research surveys. Sign up and you will automatically receive a very brief e-mailing on the day the study is released informing you of the report topic and two or three key findings. If the topic interests you, click on the link provided with the e-mail (or otherwise go to our web site) to read the entire release. We have included a "click and send" function enabling you to send the report to others whom you feel would benefit from it. (By the way, if you subscribe we will not give out your e-mail address or spam you!)

3.   Use the Data Archives. We have put hundreds of factoids and data morsels into 40 different data categories that you can access. Need facts for a sermon? Ideas on how to make a Scripture passage seem more relevant? Want to understand what people are thinking and doing in relation to a specific topic? Interested in understanding more about different segments of the population? Use this 24/7 library of faith facts whenever you're seeking a particular insight.

4.   Acquire related resources. If you are interested in additional information on specific topics, check out the reports, books, diagnostics, videos, audiotapes and other resources based on our research that is available to you. Some of these resources can be obtained only through our website.

5.   Read Barna's reviews of other valuable ministry resources. Several thousand new Christian books and related resources are produced every year. This section of the website provides reviews of recent resources to help you identify which ones might be most valuable to your own ministry and spiritual development.

We are constantly updating and expanding our website contents. We pray that you use it and profit from it. Let us know what else you want on the site. It's there for you.

www.barna.org

What Kind of Leader Are You?
Take the <u>Christian Leader Profile</u>™ and Find Out!

Have you ever wondered if you are a leader, and if you are, how you measure up?

Find out today by taking the Christian Leader Profile™. This diagnostic tool was developed by George Barna through extensive research and testing. The Profile will help you discern if and how God has called you to lead. The Profile explores four dimensions of leadership:

Has God **called you** to lead people?
Do you possess the **godly character** required of Christian leaders?
What are your strongest and weakest **leadership competencies**?
What **type of leader** are you?

It's easy and convenient to use this tool. Just logon to the Barna Research website (<u>www.barna.org</u>) and hit the icon for the Christian Leader Profile™. You will be able to take the self-administered survey online and a personalized analysis of your results will quickly be e-mailed to you. The analysis will clarify your standing as a leader and suggest future courses of action to enhance your impact for Christ through the ministry of leadership.

Be the leader that God intends you to be.
The Christian Leader Profile™ will help you become that leader.